The Personal Totem Pole:
Animal Imagery,
the Chakras,
and Psychotherapy

Eligio Stephen Gallegos, Ph.D.

Moon Bear Press 1987

THE PERSONAL TOTEM POLE

Moon Bear Press

Printing History
1st printing ....July 1987

The author gratefully acknowledges permission to reprint material from the following sources:
The Transpersonal Institute for material from "Animal Imagery, the Chakra System and Psychology, 1983, Vol. 15, No. 2, pp. 125–136, copyright 1983, © Transpersonal Institute.
The Hokuseido Press for material from "Zen in Western Literature and Oriental Classics", by R. H. Blyth, published in the U.S. by E. P. Dutton, copyright © 1942 The Hokuseido Press.

Printed in the United States of America
by
Blue Feather Press
2884 Trades West Road
Santa Fe, NM

Library of Congress Catalog Card Number: 87-90620

ISBN: 0-944164-07-2

for

All My Relations

Acknowledgements

I wish to express my deep gratitude primarily to those beautiful and warmly human clients from whose earnest desire to grow this book came into being. They well knew that in allowing me to use their very personal material they would be helping others to grow as well. "Hope!", said Sue, when I asked for her main impression of the first draft of this book, "Hope for those who so desperately need to and wish to grow."

To Mel Bucholtz who from the beginning understood the depth, significance, and value of the Personal Totem Pole process, who lent his unwavering support and continues to do so, I give my deepest thanks.

I wish to give special thanks to numerous others who in their own ways have supported and promoted the Personal Totem Pole work as well, among them Stuart Alpert, Naomi Bressette, and the staff of Hartford Family Institute, Mollie Babize, Lisa Dickson, Edie Hartshorne, Twainhart Hill, Lisa Kaye, Florence Korzinski, Winafred Lucas, Roger Luscombe, Carolyn Marks, Dorothy Mason, Bill Plotkin, Suzzanne Rosselot, Nancy Swafford, Judy Thibeau, John Vance and Edith Wallace.

And I am particularly appreciative of those beautiful people who read, edited, commented upon, and otherwise helped this manuscript, either in part or in whole, come to fruition: Richard Allen, Kacey Carmichael, Laura Chasin, Rosalie Douglas, Richard Erdoes, Kay Gallegos, T. George Harris, Dick Katz, Dolores LaChapelle, Barbara Oglesby, Johnn O'Sullivan, Teresa Rennick, Ann Roberts, Dianne Timberlake, Margaret Vasington, and Miles Vich.

Table of Contents

Chapter One
T-shirts and Totem Poles

In 1979 I took a leave of absence from the position I had held for a dozen years as Professor of Psychology in a small University and moved to the West Coast to undertake a post-doctoral residency in psychotherapy.

One of my growing interests while I taught had been the function of imagery in human growth and development, and of the use of guided imagery, or visualization, in therapy. This interest stemmed originally from the intense full dreams I had experienced from childhood, and the real dearth of understanding about their place in my life, either on my part or apparently any one else's. This had led to a study of dreams, although few people had ever really studied dreams, and to teaching several courses on the psychology of dreaming.

This, in turn, opened up my understanding of Jungian psychology, and led to my reading two books that significantly turned me to imagery. One of them was James Hillman's remarkable book called Re-Visioning Psychology. The book is his Terry Lectures delivered at Yale University in 1972 and published by Harper & Row in 1975. Brilliantly written, his thesis is that the fundamental function of the mind is to vitalize the world, by giving life and voice and awareness to all that exists, so we can listen to what the world around has to tell us and experience the world *from the perspective of each element in that world.* This is also what Fritz Perls was returning us to with Gestalt therapy. It allows those deepest elements of ourselves to participate in voice and in awareness, articulating our relationship to the world around and its relationship to us, and freeing us from the responsibility of thinking that voice and awareness belong only to that

1

particular identity that I call myself.

The other was a book by Mary Watkins called <u>Waking Dreams</u>. Researched in an attempt to understand her own imagery and later written as a Ph.D. dissertation, Watkins traces the use of imagery throughout history. The book deeply impressed me. It helped me understand not only how little we know about imagery, but also how we *as a culture* have deliberately repressed imagery: belittling it, negating it, and teaching that it has little relationship to the "real world".

So when I encountered the ad in the APA Monitor describing a postdoctoral residency in Humanistic and Holistic psychotherapy in Oregon I immediately sent off a letter expressing my interest. I was surprised to receive a call only a week later offering me the position which I accepted without hesitation.

After arriving on the West Coast I to surveyed the many growth and training workshops available and arranged to spend a week at fabled Esalen Institute, the growth center that Michael Murphy established in the 1960's which has been a leader in growth movements in our era.

I elected a Radix workshop, a system that attempts to bring one to the single root (radix in Latin) of one's emotions, mind, and body. I found the workshop informative and helpful even if the imagery involved in the process was minimal.

I was deeply refreshed by the general atmosphere at Esalen. Here was a place where growth, integration and wholeness were of primary concern. Where people looked healthy, vital, alive. Where people were willing to be open, vulnerable and receptive. Where growth into one's fullest humanness was considered the most important journey possible.

I wanted to buy a T-shirt to commemorate my inspiring stay at Esalen. Unfortunately, none of those for sale at Esalen were of my size, so I thought to myself that I would stop in San Francisco and buy one. In San Francisco I could find none that seemed to have a spirit suitable to the event. In fact, I couldn't even find a T-shirt that I liked. They all seemed to have the most unesthetic pictures of rock groups or football teams and this was hardly what Esalen was about.

I continued my search for an appropriate T-shirt and was forced to acknowledge the difficulty in finding what I thought would be a simple purchase. In utter frustration I finally bought white T-shirts and a set of Artex paints, determined to create my own tangible memory of my stay at Esalen.

My first attempt was quite simple. I used the logo from Bollingen Press: four circles seemingly emanating from a single point at the center. I drew this in black and it gave me the feel of the paints and a sense of the material. My second design was taken from a picture of an aboriginal African shield and used the colors red and blue. From here the designs became progressively more detailed and complex and I was soon involved in designs taken from the Northwest Coast Indians.

These Indians, the Nootka, Haida, Kwakiutl, Tsimshian and Coast Salish, are probably best known as the carvers of totem poles, and they are probably the finest woodcarvers in the history of mankind. The designs I began to use for my T-shirts were designs they had painted onto the front of their great wooden houses, or carved onto chests, or onto argyllite plates.

I had long been intrigued by these designs without knowing exactly why, and as I worked with them more and more I came to understand them better and to see into them more deeply. The designs are remarkably complex, highly stylized, and with some interesting consistencies among them. They are always of animals, frequently containing large numbers of elements which some contemporary artists call "ovoids" (Stewart, 1979). These are oval or round or quadrilaterals with rounded corners which seem to be used throughout the design, in the palms of the hands and soles of the feet, in the ears, eyes, belly, elbows, and kneejoints. Sometimes they are referred to as "space fillers", as if this were their main function.

As I worked more and more with these designs I suddenly became aware that these ovoids are actually eyes, and each animal characterized by these early artists is filled with eyes! It is an animal totally aware of its world; an animal that sees not only with its eyes but with its hands and feet, with its ears, with all of its joints, with its heart and belly and groin! These artists were depicting a *complete awareness!* All one need do to discover this is to see the world from the perspective of that animal, by imagining oneself as that animal and attending to the experience.

One other intriguing element occurred these designs: each animal usually contained other smaller animals as some of its components.

As I wore my T-shirts during the warmer months they came to be acknowledged by my friends and associates, and I gave a few as gifts to special people on particular occasions.

One day a client whom I had been seeing for a short while said to me, "I have a design that you may be interested in for one of your T-shirts."

I thanked her for the offer, not quite knowing what to

expect, and promptly forgot about it.

At the beginning of our next session she handed me a paper bag and I asked her what it was as it looked like someone's lunch. She told me it was the design she thought I might like for one of my T-shirts. I glanced into the bag and saw a beaded pendant done in bright orange and black and a few other colors. She told me I could keep it for awhile and I thanked her and put the bag on my desk.

Late that afternoon as I was preparing to leave the office I discovered the paper bag sitting there and again, strangely, my first thought was that someone had forgotten their lunch. As I opened the bag I was startled to see the pendant.

I took it home and began inspecting it more closely. It was a long beaded neckband that joined a circular pendant about three inches in diameter. The design was quite strange as it was not symmetrical. I had never seen an Indian pendant that was not symmetrical. Furthermore, I couldn't make out what the design was. I looked at it closely and showed it to my wife. The design seemed to represent a definite object but neither of us could tell what it was.

I became intrigued by the pendant. I set it next to my typewriter where I looked at it daily. It felt like an optical illusion that won't quite jell and which one keeps looking at not quite knowing what to do to bring it into its intended focus.

And then suddenly there it was! An eagle with wings stretched high into the sky, bursting forth out of some unknown darkness. It was so obvious that I didn't know how I had not seen it before.

I now made a large sketch of it and became very curious as to its origin. At our next session I returned the pendant to my client and asked her about it.

She had lived on an Indian reservation, she said, and when she was preparing to leave the medicine man had brought her the pendant and told her that he had made it especially for her and wanted her to take it with her when she left. She had had it ever since. I asked her if it had any meaning for her and she told me it was one of her most prized possessions. I was surprised by this because of the casual way she had brought it in a paper bag and left it with me. She could tell me nothing more about it.

In our therapy session that day I conducted her through a visualization which is frequently used in Psychosynthesis. In it a person is guided to find a path which leads to a cave in the side of a mountain. Deep within there is a brightly illuminated chamber where a wise old being sits, someone with whom one can communicate about the important aspects of one's life and growth. This being represents the "higher self" (Miller, 1978).

My client described herself initially as walking through the woods. After searching around she found a path that led out of the woods and to the mountain. It was a bright sunlit day as she made her way along the path. She then said to me, "Up ahead the path turns sharply to the right and I can see something there where it turns but I can't tell what it is."

I asked her to continue along the path suggesting that as she came closer she might recognize it.

She then said, "Oh, it's a totem pole with a number of animals carved on it. I can see that the top animal is an eagle and there's one right below it but I can't tell what it is, and the next one's a bear, and there are several others below the bear but I can't see them clearly enough to make out what they are."

She followed the turning path and continued on until she reached the cave in the mountain, entered it and met a wise old being who was seated in the center of a large chamber.

They engaged in a lengthy conversation and when they were through our session was also over.

She left, taking the pendant with her, and even though we had a session scheduled for the following week, I never saw this woman again.

Later that same day, while jogging through the hills above town, this entire situation kept tugging at my mind. I was thinking about the totem pole and the abrupt turn in the path when I suddenly understood that the totem pole was me and that I was a signpost at a turning point in my clients path.

I also experienced the instantaneous realization that the bear was my heart and the eagle my head, and I could feel them in those places in my body. As I continued jogging I realized that these two animals, in some way, also represented my fourth and sixth chakras. I thought to myself, "I wonder what my other animals are", and, as I focussed in my body, I could see quite clearly, and in a few cases surprisingly, my throat animal, solar plexus animal, gut animal, and grounding animal. I was so intrigued by this and by the obvious appropriateness of the animals in these places within me that I began exploring this procedure with my clients and friends the very next day.

Chapter Two
Power Centers and Animals

The only reason I knew anything about chakras at this time was because I had participated in a number of group therapy sessions with a sensitive and skillful therapist named Ma Prem Mala. She had recently returned from India where she had been studying.

She was the first therapist I had met who consistently brought a person to a sense of completion at each session of her work with them. To hear her describe it, she would tune in to where the energy was and participate in whatever needed to happen in order for the energy to move to a new point of stabilization.

Mala taught me that there were concentrations of energy located in different areas of the body. There are seven of these power centers located along the body midline and each center is related to certain emotional or psychological functions, or processes of action.

Mala was able to look at each of these power centers in a person and tell what was happening with the energy there. She called these centers "chakras", a sanskrit term meaning wheel. This ancient perspective describes the human being as comprised of different "wheels" of energy. In the healthy individual, each chakra should be open and clear, with the energy able to flow freely. If a chakra is blocked the person will be incapable of efficiently utilizing the energy at that level, and will experience a certain deficiency or even physical illness. For a person to be healthy, both physically and psychologically, every chakra must be open and capable of processing energy efficiently. And each chakra is related to a characteristic aspect of being.

She taught me that the first center is located at the base of the spine in the middle of the perineum. When it is healthy a person experiences a solid sense of security and a wholesome relationship to the earth and to nature.

The second one is located just below the navel, in what the Japanese call the "hara" or what we call the gut or belly. It's domain is the passions and emotions. When it is fully functional the person is fully aware of their feelings and is emotionally expressive.

The third is in the solar plexus and is related to one's personal power. This is not the typical Western view of power which is so heavily masculinized as control, force, or coercion, but the power to act, cleanly, deliberately, effectively.

The fourth is centered in the heart and is concerned with love, compassion, community.

The fifth is in the throat and is the power center of communication and expression.

The sixth is located in the forehead and is sometimes known as the "third eye". It is related to the intellect and intuition.

The seventh is located at the very top of the head is concerned with the relationship to one's spirit.

This was originally a difficult concept for me as a Westerner to grasp, with my extensive training in scientific method and Behaviorism. When introduced to the chakras the first thing a Westerner does is look for structural underpinnings. "What is it really?" So we try to envision it in terms of underlying neural plexuses or glandular systems: something objective that we are comfortable with. But the fact is that the chakra system emanates from a particular *subjective* exploration of the body. These energies are perceptually tangible to those who have gone through the necessary training. I had great difficulty accepting this view and understanding that it had any more than a descriptive meaning. Until I met the animals.

When I first met my power animals as I was jogging that evening, several things either were significant or later became significant. First, there was no Spiritual animal, although I didn't even notice it at the time. There was no question but that my head chakra, or my third eye, was an Eagle and my heart was a bear. These were the only two animals clearly visible to my client in the totem pole she saw at the turning point in her path, and the eagle was definitely the top animal. Because of this, in my ensuing work I dealt with only the first six chakras and for a year did not seek the spiritual animal either in myself or in people with whom I worked. I will return to this topic later.

Second, all my animals were powerful except for my grounding animal, a rabbit. I immediately chuckled because I was jogging along and had the feeling of those long rabbit feet powerfully pressing forth. But I was also aware of the rabbit as a relatively weak and timid animal. And it was certainly the smallest of my animals. I didn't like to think of myself as timid, but I had to acknowledge that was an element I had long possessed and tried to hide.

Over the next few days I began to deeply experience the fact that even though I had involved myself seriously in education and in educating myself for much of my life, I was insecure, I did not have a sense of myself as strongly related to nature and the natural world. I became poignantly aware of myself as separate and not well grounded, not strongly rooted.

I had also been thinking about the chakra system and

wondering how it related to a group of animals. What would be the animal equivalent of all chakras fully functioning in relation to each other? In the chakra system it would mean each chakra being open and healthy, fully processing its energy, and allowing this energy to flow freely between all chakras. For the animals I had the sense that this would entail all the animals being fully free and healthy, and living in open harmony with each other. So I invited all of my animals to come together in a council meeting.

They willingly agreed and gathered together under a large old Live Oak tree. I was surprised to see that few of them had met before. As they gathered they formed a circle and the rabbit looked at the others and began telling them how small and weak he felt in their presence, how afraid he was of them because they were all large and powerful.

As the rabbit spoke a memory came to me of a time when I was five years old. I had been in kindergarten for several weeks. My mother, a teacher, had prepared me well for school and I was enjoying my competence. One day the teacher came over to me and said, "You're much too smart to be in here. You really should be in the first grade," whereupon she took me by the arm and led me down a long hallway to the first grade classroom. Where the kindergarten class had consisted of a dozen children, the first grade class held thirty. And they were all bigger and older than I. I felt dwarfed, highly inadequate and tremendously lonely. The feeling of not really belonging hit me with a powerful impact. I recognized this feeling had been with me all my life.

Then each animal in turn told the rabbit how much they appreciated and loved it. They also assured it that it was definitely one of them and that it belonged among them. The rabbit was deeply touched by their kindness and acceptance.

11

They all offered their support and urged the rabbit to grow to be their equal. At this the rabbit suddenly began growing larger and larger until it was a giant rabbit about ten feet tall. The other animals stood back in appreciation and the rabbit became very still and settled, no longer afraid, and with a deep sense of belongingness.

I was amazed to observe this. As it was growing I personally experienced my old feeling of not belonging, of being small and weak, draining away. I felt a new sense of ease. And I subsequently began to feel much more settled in my own life and pursuits. And I felt a deep appreciation for the rabbit and for the support the other animals had offered it.

I also developed a renewed interest in totem poles: What was their significance? Why were they carved? What was the origin of these Northwest Coast Natives? Is it possible that the totem poles were in fact representative of the chakra energies? How did the Northwest Coast Indians relate to animals? Did the totem poles and modern chakra theory have a common origin?

Chapter Three
The Dead Dog

At the time I first discovered the animals in the power centers I was working at a small mental health clinic. I had quit my academic job and taken some time off to co-author a book with a friend, Teresa Rennick. We had met at the Center where I was a resident. She also knew the potency of guided imagery and taught a course on Imagery and Healing at the local college where she was a faculty member in the Department of Nursing.

We were interested in writing a book in which guided imagery was allowed to stand on its own, without any need to translate it into another dimension. We felt imagery was itself foundational, and that to translate it into some equivalence tended to diminish its inherent integrity and position. Imagery is not valuable because of what it means, its value precedes conceptual meaning, or exists "in relation to" but not "reducible to" concepts, even though concepts may be applied to different aspects of imagery. Inner Journeys: Visualization in Growth and Therapy, was published in 1984 by Turnstone Press Ltd.

One of my clients at that time was a woman who I will call Jane. She had been in group therapy for the past five years, since first experiencing a "nervous breakdown". Her symptoms were depression, self-negation, and extreme suicidal tendencies. Her previous therapists had encouraged her to enter into "non-suicide" contracts with them and she admitted to me at the end of our therapy that she had restipulated the contract almost daily in order to keep from attempting suicide.

Jane was 34 years old, divorced, with two children. Her manner was intense and her voice high pitched. The first time I met with the group she expressed a fear of me. I assured her that I respected her and trusted her ability to grow, and that I would do nothing to threaten or pressure her, which she accepted. She told me at the time that she hated herself because she wasn't perfect. I told her that I felt each human being was a beautiful flower deep inside. She replied that she was sure there was no flower within herself. I had the group do a visualization to get in touch with the inner flower. Jane expressed surprise at what she had seen: a tiny baby.

At our next meeting I heard more of her history. She had grown up on a remote ranch in northern Wyoming. Her mother was dominating, usually angry, and defensive. Jane felt she had never been good enough for her mother and that she had not been wanted from the time she was born. Her older sister had a personality similar to that of her mother. Her father was passive and quiet.

She said she felt like she was nothing; her existence was a deep dark well with a lid over it. The only delight she had experienced in her early life was when her father took her hunting or fishing with him. Although he seldom said anything, on these occasions she felt that he truly cared for her. When I asked if she could give each of these little girls a different name, this one she called "Richness." The other's name was "Nothing."

She also expressed a tendency to want to withdraw into a corner where she would be safe. I assured her she was free to retreat to the corner whenever she wished, as she was also free to come out of that corner. I encouraged her to practice both of these movements so they could both become voluntary.

At our next session I asked her to place the chairs in the room to represent the positions of family members at home. Mother and sister chairs were placed in the center of the room, her own and her father's were placed in two corners. As a newborn baby her position had been at the center of the room, but sitting in that position she immediately felt jealousy from her mother and sister. As she removed herself to the corner her father also moved to a corner in silent support of her.

In the following session I used guided imagery to bring the members of the group into contact with their power animals. The animal in Jane's forehead (Intellectual/Intuitive) was a giant eagle. Jane was standing below it and could only see its legs and lower body. Its first words were to tell her how dumb and stupid she was. She was shocked by this and asked it why it was saying such things. It replied that it wanted to give her an example of what she does to herself.

The animal in her throat (Communication) was a weasel. Jane felt demeaned at this, but there was an understanding that perhaps she used communication in attempts to weasel out of some things.

The animal in her heart (Love/Compassion) was a dead dog encrusted with a fungal growth, lying on a stone slab in a cave. The dog had obviously been dead for a long while. Jane was visibly shaken by this. So was I. My question to myself was, "Does this mean that she's going to commit suicide?"

The animal in her solar plexus (Power) was a white bird in a cage. The bird asked Jane to open the door and release it. She did as requested and when it emerged from the cage it turned into a large dragon, roaring in anguish. Jane, terrified, immediately seized it, shoved it back into the cage and closed the door whereupon it once again became a white bird.

The animal in her gut (Emotion) was a small fuzzy bear who reached inside of Jane and removed a small blue stone which he held up. A soft blue glow emanated from the stone which illuminated the entire room with a good feeling.

Her Grounding animal was a playful porpoise.

In my thinking about the chakra system in relation to the animals up until now, I had come to the understanding that the equivalent of a closed or limited chakra was represented by an animal that was injured, caged, or in some way not functioning optimally. In terms of Jane's animals this meant that her Power chakra was closed (the white bird in the cage) . But when it was open the state and size of her power severely frightened her (the dragon). Furthermore, I had some serious questions about the dead dog. One of them was, "Does this mean that her heart chakra is totally dead and incapable of ever functioning again? Is she completely dead to ever experiencing love or compassion again? If so, what now?"

As I had done with my own animals, I asked Jane to invite her animals to gather together so that they themselves could assess the circumstances and decide on what action needed to be taken. The white bird told her that it would have to be released from it's cage in order to attend the council meeting. She reluctantly opened the cage door and allowed it to emerge. Again it turned into a dragon, roaring. Jane suddenly became aware that it wasn't roaring so much as wailing; wailing over the dog being dead.

As the animals gathered, they met in the cave and formed a circle around the dead dog as it lay on the stone slab. As they stood there, Jane among them, she suddenly became aware of the presence of a small baby and a fifteen year old boy. I watched as she burst into uncontrolled sobbing.

"That's the baby that I was pregnant with when I was nineteen! I had an abortion! I shouldn't have done that! It was completely wrong! It was terrible of me to have the abortion! I shouldn't have done it! I shouldn't have done it!"

This was the first I had known of the abortion.

She knew that the fifteen year old boy was the baby had it been born. The boy turned to her and said, "It's okay. I'm content where I am. You did what you needed to do at the time and I'm not angry at you. Now you need to accept the fact that you had the abortion and not judge yourself."

She again burst into tears. "No! It was wrong! I shouldn't have done it! I shouldn't have done it! I killed that little baby!"

The boy and all the animals now looked at her compassionately but firmly and said, "You need to accept the fact that you had the abortion."

Again she railed, "I can't! I can't! It was wrong of me to do that!"

Again, calmly and firmly, they reiterated, "You need to accept it."

There was no coercion on the part of the animals, and no attempt to force Jane in any way. Yet they were firmly of one mind.

After a bout of prolonged crying Jane quietly said, "All right. I accept it. I had the abortion."

At this the dog suddenly returned to life. It's coat became sleek and shiny, and it went and stood at Jane's side. The dragon stopped its wailing. And the weasel turned into a swan.

Her voice was no longer high pitched, but had a new softness as she said, "I guess I've condemned myself enough. I was only a kid." All of the animals celebrated the dog's return to life, and the baby and boy were gone.

Jane was astonished and deeply moved. So was I. I was also relieved.

Chapter Four
My Name is Richness

Jane continued to be amazed and joyful at the return of her dog. And she came to experience a deep love for all her animals, feeling that they were always with her, within her, accompanying her.

Then one day she was visibly upset. Her dragon, by whom she had been initially so terrifed, was beginning to change. She had grown to love him so and now he was beginning to change. She didn't want that. She liked him as a dragon and wanted to keep him as he was. He had already lost his scales, his body had become rather hairy, and she knew his legs were growing longer. She was very sad at this and demanded that he stop changing, which he dutifully did, but then all the animals became passive and unresponsive. And she was feeling very depressed and upset.

I talked to her for awhile about the need to let go. About the fact that growing involves change, and change involves letting go of the old so there can be room for the new. I also spoke to her of the pain and sadness of letting go of someone we love, and of the need to be willing to openly experience those painful emotions without trying to hold them at bay. She told me she had always had difficulty letting go of people and things that she loved. I explained that letting go does not mean stopping to love but ceasing to cling. She finally acknowledged that her attempt to cling to the dragon as he had been was making things miserable, and in fact, he was already different so it was futile anyway. She agreed to let him go.

In the visualization which we then did, Jane met with her dragon who was now rather bedraggled, and he told her that he was leaving. She said goodbye and watched as he went over a hill. I encouraged Jane allow herself to fully experience the sadness of letting go and she cried. This was the very first time she had ever *voluntarily* let go of anything she loved.

A few moments later a brown winged horse flew toward her. She knew that this was her power animal transformed. He took her for a ride to a distant valley where she found a small girl named Richness who was herself.

A month later Jane came to see me in a private session. She told me that her thoughts of suicide had become very intense of late. As we talked she revealed to me that these thoughts had always been accompanied by a feeling of terror. Upon closer questioning she revealed something that she herself had apparently not realized until then: that she would *first* feel the terror and *then* her thoughts would go immediatey to suicide. We agreed to meet the following week to do a visualization in which she would encounter her terror directly, and I asked her to reconfirm her non-suicide commitment.

When we met the next week she told me she had not wanted to come see me but knew she must. She had not slept for the past several nights and the feeling of terror had been almost always present.

In the visualization I asked her to first meet with the animals. They gathered together in the cave and I suggested she ask them if this would be an appropriate time to encounter her terror. They all acknowledged that the time was propitious except for the eagle (Intellect/Intuition) who remained silent. She then asked if they would support her in the encounter and they all said they would.

I asked Jane to allow her terror to present itself to her

as an image. It appeared immediately as a large, bearded man wearing a black hat and cracking a whip, menacingly. He looked much like her father except that her father had no beard.

She asked him why he was cracking the whip.

"So you'll be afraid!", he replied.

"What do you want of me?", she asked.

"I want you to disappear!"

I suggested she ask him if he would be willing to give her his energy for her growth and he answered that he would not.

I then suggested she ask him to tell her when he had first appeared in her life.

She immediately saw herself as a very small child, together with her sister, jumping up and down on a bed, making noise and having fun. Her mother was sick in an adjacent bedroom. Her father suddenly appeared in the doorway, enraged. He removed his belt and whipped them both, leaving welts and blisters on her small body.

Jane was startled and shaken by this apparent memory. I instinctively asked her to take whichever animals she wished and return to that early scene to heal those two girls and the father. She took the dog (Love/Compassion) and the flying horse (Power) with her. The dog licked both girls' wounds, healing them, and the flying horse healed the father of his rage.

She then returned to the cave with the animals where Terror was also waiting. He was now tiny. She asked again if he would give her his energy for her growth. He refused and grew big again.

I suggested she ask him to show her the second time he came into her life.

She saw a scene of herself as a small child, perhaps two years old, with her hands tied behind her back. Many people were around but she didn't know what was going on.

I suggested that she see the scene just prior to this.

It was at her parents home. It was a party. She went to the bathroom by herself, proud that she was doing so by herself for the first time, but she emerged without her panties. Her parents were shocked, spanked her, and tied her hands behind her back. She didn't understand why they were upset as she thought she was doing something good.

I again suggested that she return to the scene, taking any animals that she wished, to heal the little girl and her parents. She took the swan (Communication) and the bear (Emotion), and at the last minute the dog (Love/Copmpassion) came along also.

So many people were present making such noise that she couldn't seem to do anything. At this the swan honked at them and kept them occupied while she untied the girls hands and she and the dog soothed her. The bear had both parents lie on the floor, unzippered their chests and with his blue jewel erased something from their hearts.

Upon returning to the cave Terror was still present so I suggested she ask him to show her the third time he had come into her life. She then saw numerous events of chastisement, punishment, and rejection, sequentially, as if they were being projected onto the wall of the cave. I suggested she ask all the animals to stand with her and shine a healing light from their hearts onto the scenes. They did.

When the scenes were over Terror was gone. The whip was lying on the floor. And her father, clean shaven, hat in hand, was standing before them staring at the floor. The animals told her that she needed to unravel the whip and macrame it into a wall hanging. She was loathe to do this so I suggested that perhaps her father would be willing to help. He was.

Together they unravelled the whip and spent some time with the macrame. When they were done, Jane suddenly said, "My God! This is the same wall hanging I made five years ago when I was in the hospital!"

All the animals then danced in celebration with Jane and her father.

When the session was over Jane told me that she did not remember the two events and that they had certainly not happened to her as a child. I said that it didn't matter whether they were factual events or not. Obviously something in her had changed, been healed, as she was no longer experiencing terror, and that is what mattered.

When I saw her two weeks later she expressed amazement that there had been no further thoughts of suicide. She said it felt very strange to her because for the previous five years not a day had passed that she had not thought of suicide.

There was a clear, direct look in her eye. Her voice was calm and settled. She told me that her friends had commented on how changed she looked. She also told me that the small fuzzy bear had now grown to full size, and each of her animals had a blue, glowing jewel in its heart. She felt deeply joyful.

Three months later she visited her sister who lived in a nearby city, and without mentioning anything directly she asked her sister if she remembered anything painful that had happened to them as children. The sister immediately began talking about the time they had been whipped for jumping on the bed when their mother was sick.

Chapter Five
Journeys

In June of 1983 I travelled to Vancouver, British Columbia, to present a paper at the annual meeting of the American Association for the Study of Mental Imagery. This was the first formal statement of what I had by now come to call the **Personal Totem Pole** process and I was pleased to be able to present it first in the region where the totem pole carvers themselves had lived.

It was my first attendance at a gathering of the organization which was relatively new as this was only their fifth annual meeting.

My own talk was scheduled at the same time as that of Jerome L. Singer of Yale University and only about a dozen people were present as I began.

I had been struck at this meeting by the large number of papers that were extremely academic and which attempted to fit imagery into the traditional mold of scientific research, with statistical analyses, frequency counts, etc., which greatly missed the aliveness and creative richness that gives imagery it's individual uniqueness. But I was also aware that most of these people had been trained in the traditional psychological model where scientific method is seen as a *foundation* rather than just one among many *tools*. My own academic training and early research had also been in this mold, probably even more so than that of most of those present. My Ph.D. dissertation had been an electrophysiological investigation into some properties of the temperature receptors in the skin of cats and monkies, a study that could as easily have been performed in the departments of physiology or biophysics.

I began by saying to the small group that I was going

to speak to them as a therapist not as a scientist and I began to describe the story of my therapeutic association with Jane. As I spoke more and more people drifted into the rather large hall until a large group was present. I later discovered that Dr. Singer had not appeared for his talk, having left a phone message with the hotel desk clerk concerning his intended absence that had never been delivered, and so I happened to "inherit" his audience. My talk was well received, there were numerous questions from the audience, and considerable interest was expressed in my approach. Two physicians in psychiatric residency and one psychologist aproached me to do a short experiential session with them which was accomplished at the end of the meeting.

After leaving the meeting in Vancouver I stopped in Portland, Oregon to visit Ma Prem Mala whom I had not seen since before my discovery of the chakra animals. Over coffee I described extensively my work with the chakra animals and the circumstances of their discovery. When I had finished she remained silent for a long while and then said softly, "That pendant was a key, and it needed to unlock something in you so you could receive the message the woman was carrying. She delivered the message and that's why she didn't return to see you again. Her job was done. She was a only a messenger and probably didn't realize the significance, or even the nature, of the message she delivered."

It was strange to hear this, and at the same time comforting. I myself had felt that this process was not something I had invented or created, but something very ancient which was now being handed back to us. And I felt honored to be one of the vehicles by means of which it arrived again in the world.

I also wrote an article which I submitted to the *Journal of Transpersonal Psychology*. I had originally entitled the article "The Personal Totem Pole" and although I didn't describe the specific way in which I had been introduced to the process I did potentially attribute the process to the Northwest Coast Indians.

Some months later I received a phone call from Dr. Miles Vich, the editor of the Journal. He told me the article had been put through their editorial review process and that it had been well received but there were some questions about the appropriateness of the relationship of the process to the Northwest Coast Indians. I agreed that nothing had been verified, that this relationship was not essential to the working or understanding of the process, and that I would be content to omit it at this point and research the question in more depth. Dr. Vich was friendly and cordial; his directness and sincerity left me with a good feeling.

I was surprised when I soon after received a copy of my article which included proposed editorial changes. Most of the changes were appropriate and enhanced my original attempts at writing, but I was perplexed to see that it included a negative statement about the relationship of this process to more "primitive" cultures. What had been included as a final paragraph was:

"It is also important to point out that this symbolic and metaphoric use of animals is quite different from primitive identification with animals as practiced in animistic and totemistic cultures. The purpose of the above described procedure is to aid and assist the client to become free of conditioned responses, neurotic patterns, and similar limitations and grow toward increasing awareness and full development of psychological and spiritual capacities. *This is a strikingly different aim than that of a religious or socially enforced identification with a tribal totemic animal spirit. While the evocative power of animal imagery may be strong in either a totemic or a contemporary therapeutic use of imagination, the differences in cultural context, intentions and outcomes necessarily lead in different psychological directions"* (my italics).

I was perplexed because this statement was the opposite of my thoughts on the subject, and though admittedly my familiarity with anthropological studies of totemic cultures was meager, I had an intuitive sense that the portion which I have italicized was incorrect. I felt that particularly the use of animal imagery, art, and costume as practiced by the Northwest Coast Indians was a means of growing beyond a narrow ego, a mode of expansion into a more full humanness. And I can only say that I felt this through the aliveness and awareness expressed in their art.

I agonized over this editorial inclusion for days. On the one had I felt that it was important that my article be published so that other therapists and professionals could begin to explore this dimension of growth. On the other hand I felt that to include this paragraph would be to state something that I not only did not believe, but it would be a statement of the opposite of what I felt to be the case.

I finally called Miles and told him of my concern. I said I felt the use of animals was significant in the psychological growth of the peoples of the Northwest Coast, that it was indicated in their art, in the depiction of a number of carved animal being portrayed in stages of *tranformation* from one animal into another; that their cultural rituals involved them dressing as various animals and ritually becoming those animals; that their culture was based on a high valuation of *conscious awareness,* and that ultimately they were strongly *shamanistic.* And if shamanism is concerned with anything it is concerned with transformation. Miles was completely understanding and I felt that this editorial inclusion did not come from him but from some other member of the editorial board. We agreed it would be best to just omit the paragraph entirely.

The article was published as "Animal imagery, the chakra system, and psychotherapy" in the Winter 1983 issue. It was obviously well received as numerous requests for reprints began arriving and many letters from professional people around the world. Several therapists began employing it with their clients, wrote to tell me of the results, and praised the approach.

After my article was written I was encouraged by my friend, Mel Bucholtz, a therapist in Cambridge, Massachusets, who had read the article, to travel to Boston to conduct a workshop at Interface Institute where he is a faculty member. He helped clear the way with the directors and in January 1984 I visited Boston.

At a gathering of invited guests at Mel's apartment he asked me to give a short talk about my approach. In introducing me he said:

> I want to introduce a very good friend and colleague, Steve Gallegos, and I'd like to tell you what I see in what Steve is doing.
>
> It seems to me an extremely important merging of a lot of different approaches in poetics and esthetics, as well as what I've come to be aware of in Milton Erikson's trance work in really deep learning. Over the past couple of

days I have made some notes, and some of the people who have contributed to them are here, like Dennis and Barbara Tedlock. They have done some magnificent work with regard to what the American Indian can offer to us to help shape our awareness of what consciousness change can be about in a very real, very personal way. You may be able to see in your own way, how what I find interesting in Steve's work is what looks to me like the first truly 100% indigenous psychology, that is to say a kind of psychology that seems to just come from being here physically.

We are all familiar with inputs from the Orient, inputs from Europe, thinking conceptually, and this is such an extremely simple approach, which is evoked naturally from the unconsicous that when I first encountered it I discovered that I was shocked later. You know, when you find something that's so true you're not really so amazed by it at the moment, but later on you say, "That really is quite good, isn't it?", but it's later. And that's what I found in the work that Steve introduced to me.

One thing that comes to mind is a little known lecture of C. G. Jung called "Mind and the Earth". It's a fabulously interesting thing which Jung talked about when he visited the States in 1912, when he went to Clark University in Worcester. He went with a doctor friend of his to Buffalo, New York, and is standing at the gate of a foundry and while watching the workers file out Jung says to the fellow, "Most of these people are American Indian," and his friend turns to him and says "I don't think that there's maybe ten of them that are American Indian at all". And Jung then uses that as a starting point to say that he feels there's a kind of an Indianization of American consciousness. The reason that he gets to that is that in working with a lot of his American clients, he noticed that there was a way of moving, a way of symbolizing, that in no way bore any resemblance to the way his European clients symbolized their experience. Jung was talking about an inherited legacy of American Indian consciousness that seems to come through the people that live here. So that just being here on this terrain dictates a kind of symbolism through the body to negotiate simply being here.

And this is very foreign to us to comprehend: that the earth directly influences the way the mind functions and symbolizes experience.

Dennis Tedlock did a beautiful piece called "The Way of the Word of the Breath". And this piece, to my mind, reflected also the evolution of American poetry which talks so much about the quality of breathing. And breathing, after all, as you pointed out, is an indication or an index of the quality of the condition of the heart and the lungs, and they, themselves, are an indication of the whole body. So if we go back into church music we find inspirational music, or cantatas, or chanting, are a statement about the quality of the breath as the breath reveals the condition of the individual. So this again came to mind as Steve and I were talking. How does the breath reveal the quality of the person and the life the person has lived?

One thing I noticed about Steve's work is that it started at the end point of what I call Western Psychologies, which mostly deal with ego. Part of the reason it's so exciting to me is that it involves a transcendent quality, which of course informs immediate behavior.

And then I was thinking of Ram Dass's statement that "you only get as high as your therapist is." Which is really quite an important statement. Of course as Picasso points out, where the student comes to Picasso and says to him, "Do you think I'll ever be as good as you are?" and Picasso says, "You fool, you'd better be better than I am! I'm teaching you at 74 and you're 23 years old!"

So there is this kind of a quality that something far

beyond where you are in terms of materiality and ego has to guide or direct the learning. If you're only doing it at the point of the ego, all the work that's done is patchwork, solving an immediate problem, and so on and so forth. And those of us who work clinically know that. You're only solving an immediate issue, or dealing with symptoms, or however you want to describe it.

This leads me into talking about one other reference to D. T. Suzuki from R. H. Blyth, who deals with Haiku poetry which he sees as the ultimate expression of the fruition of Oriental thought as it reaches its apogee: the point at which it produces action. He says, "we grasp the inexpressible meaning of some quite ordinary thing or fact hitherto entirely overlooked. Haiku is the apprehension of the thing by the realization of our own original essential unity with it. The word realization having the literal meaning here of "making real in ourselves". The thing perceives itself in us; we perceive it by simple self-consciousness. The joy of the apparent reunion in ourselves with things, with all things, is thus the happiness of being our true selves. It is with "all things", because as Dr. Suzuki explains on his works on Zen, when one thing is taken up, all things are taken up with it. One flower is the Spring, a falling leaf has the whole of Autumn, of every Autumn, of the eternal, the timeless Autumn of each thing and of all things."

What I find so incredible about that is the <u>sense of recovery</u>. To recover what animates oneself, that organizes experience. In my work, as some of you know, I feel that the esthetic is what organizes the unconscious into conscious activity. What Steve has done, and part of the importance of it is, it leaves it to the person directly, and it does so in a way that's so elegantly simple and accurate that it seemed to me to come directly from the way the American Indian understood the relationship of the Self to the forms and forces of the natural world. An extremely elementary, very simple, yet extremely sophisticated way of understanding how to comprehend oneself in relation to the environment which keeps some fundamental issues intact: how to keep the sense of self intact while being in contact with the world, how to comprehend the nature of relationship, whether it be to immediate human family or extended animal family and extended plant family, extended environmental family; so that there is connection all the way through. And these are some of the elements I saw when Steve and I first began to talk, when he told me "Well, I've wandered onto these animal sort of things", you know, in his incredibly offhand manner, "it seems sort of interesting and I'm not exactly sure what it means," and I sat there for a couple of days and I thought, "Gee, I wonder what it means?" and I said, "What it means?, I think I get the point, Steve, I know what it means. And so I'm really very happy that I could have some time to take with you to be with Steve and with his work and I've asked him if he would be willing to tell us about how it came together for him and about the specific work that illustrated the kinds of things I saw and things that he sees in addition, which are so natural in a person healing themselves. And it's a total system, it's not just parts putting it together, the system puts itself together in a natural Gestalt, so magnificently, that I just haven't seen anything quite like it.

While in Boston I presented two workshops, one at Interface Institute and a second for the Institute of Neurolinguistic Programming. It was bitterly cold in Boston and I had not brought adequate clothing. A cold wave known as the "Siberian Express" was sweeping down from the Arctic. I caught cold but nonetheless the workshops went very well. In fact, several therapists present at the workshops subsequently began to employ the animal chakras in their work.

Before I present a workshop I always contact my animals and ask their advice on what I should do at the workshop and I request their support. Before leaving Oregon for Boston my heart animal had changed from a bear into a giant white lotus blossom that was closed. It looked like a large translucent globe. My animals, very tiny in relation to the lotus, were all sitting in a circle inside it like little seeds.

As Mel was driving me to the second workshop I checked back in with my animals and felt a deep deep wave of emotion as I saw that the lotus had blossomed and the animal seeds were spewing out over the city of Boston.

Chapter Six
Raising the Puppies

Mary was a young professional who came to see me because she was asked by her supervisor to seek counselling for apparent difficulty in communication. She told me that she was surprised by the request, feeling that she communicated adequately. Indeed, she was open and direct with me. She did tell me that she felt intimidated by her supervisor and generally held back from authority, feeling that it was not up to her to step in if someone in authority were present. The appearance she presented was of a sensitive and intelligent young lady who perhaps frequently knew more than her supervisor but for cultural reasons had learned early not to appear more knowledgeable than an authority figure. My first thought was that she could benefit from assertiveness training.

Mary also informed me that at the age of four she had been playing with matches early one morning when the pants she was wearing became ignited and burst into flame, badly burning both legs. This resulted in lengthy stays in hospitals over the next several years as she underwent numerous skin grafts. As her family lived on a farm two hundred miles from the nearest hospital, she was separated from them for long periods of time. She also told me that in high school she had felt somewhat "paranoid".

She was open and receptive and very willing to grow. In order to test her imagery I asked her to imagine that she was a seed that had been in the frozen earth through a long winter. Gradually Spring arrives and the earth begins to thaw. A warm gentle rain falls, soaking into the earth. The seed sends roots into the earth and grows into a flower that blossoms.

Mary's image was of fine threadlike roots growing

deep into rich soil, a thick, strong stem with some thorns, and a delicate white flower with eight petals. It said to her, "I'll blossom for you but don't pick me. Learn to share with me what I need."

The next two sessions were spent in making contact with her chakra animals.

Mary's Intellectual/Intuitive animal was a fox who lived in a cave. Its name was Anger and it told her that it didn't like being caged up. When asked who had caged it, it replied that everyone did. It told her that it wanted people to know that it could do good things, that it was not all bad.

Her Communication animal was an owl named Hooty that looked like a cartoon caricature. It told Mary that things could be fun, they don't always have to be terribly serious.

Her Love/Compassion animal was a beautiful dove, named Dove. It told her to be at peace, and also that she needed to know she was not like everyone else, that she was an individual and needed to accept the fact.

Her Power animal was a turtle named Toby. It told Mary to be patient, that sometimes she got too busy and she needed to stop and look at the little things.

Her Emotional animal was a terrier that had just given birth to a litter of four puppies. It picked them up individually and carried them to Mary, placed them in her lap, and asked her to feed them, take care of them, and love them. When the terrier was asked what it needed, it replied that its only need was to know Mary's love through the puppies. It told Mary the names of the puppies (Joey, Bernard, Bernice, and Pal) and then left, never to return. Mary cried.

Mary's Grounding animal was a giraffe named Paul who expressed his happiness at seeing her. She asked if he would go with her to meet the other animals and form a council. He agreed. She took him to meet the puppies and left him with them. She then went to see the turtle and asked if it would come join the others. It replied that since it was so slow it would make its way to the puppies while she gathered the remaining animals. She then went to the dove who agreed to come and rode on her right shoulder. They both then went to meet the owl who complimented the dove on its beauty. The three of them then went to meet the fox. He was distant and hesitant, and told Mary that he felt she didn't like him as well as she liked the owl and dove. She was saddened by this and praised the fox, telling him that she did in fact appreciate him. They all went to meet the puppies. When they arrived the turtle was already there. The owl and the turtle got along very well.

At our fourth session Mary was more settled and talkative than she had previously been, discussing her family, her views of her profession and ideas she had for making it more responsive to human needs. We did a brief visualization where she went to see her animals. She was met first by Paul the giraffe (her Grounding animal). He told her that things needed to be better organized and that some of the other animals needed to assume greater responsibility for the puppies. All the animals were present except for the owl (Communication), who then appeared. The giraffe suggested that the owl and the dove (Love/Compassion) could assume greater responsibility for feeding the puppies (Emotion). They both agreed to do this and Mary then noticed that the owl looked more dignified than it had during the previous session.

The turtle (Power) told Mary that he was afraid of me. I asked her to assure him that I would not ask him to do anything for which he was not ready, and that I trusted him to grow when he was ready. He spontaneously agreed to assume responsibility for cleaning the basket that the puppies were in and immediately began to do so, even decorating it with flowers which he gathered.

The fox (Intellect/Intuition) was particularly fascinated by the puppies. One in particular was very friendly with him. He agreed to help by watching the puppies while the turtle cleaned the basket . The giraffe suggested that the fox could also wash the puppies by licking them like a mother dog. He agreed to do this.

The dove was more concerned with caring about the other animals than about herself.

Mary noticed that the puppies eyes were now open. She asked them how she could help them grow and they replied, "By coming to visit us!" All the animals then gathered around and hummed or sang to the puppies as they fell asleep.

At the beginning of our fifth session Mary told me of a vivid dream she had during the previous week. She dreamt that she was asleep in her house and something entered which didn't belong there. She didn't know what it was as she couldn't see it, but she could feel it, and she chased it out of the house.

During the day following the dream another curious event occurred: Mary began spontaneously visualizing a meeting with her animals. Suddenly two swans arrived, one black and one white, offering to build a new house for the puppies if they would be allowed to join the group. Although the owl was accepting of them none of the other animals were, and they treated the swans with suspicion. Mary told them that they would not be allowed to join the group and that they would have to leave. As they left they turned into lizard-like creatures surrounded by a putrid smell. Mary reported this to me in wonder, feeling that she had been correct in rejecting them. I did not pursue the matter any further.

Mary reported one other event that had occurred since our previous meeting. She had been standing in her kitchen when she spontaneously had the following visualization: the turtle began growing very rapidly and then suddenly exploded. Pieces of turtle shell littered the floor and an elephant was standing in its place. This was her new power animal.

I asked Mary to meet with the animals in council and ask them to discuss among themselves which of them most needed to grow next. The dove suggested that the fox most needed to grow. The owl suggested that the fox not grow yet so that it could still spend some time with the puppies, and the giraffe agreed that this was a good idea. They then suggested to the dove that he be the one to grow. He agreed.

I had Mary ask the dove if he knew what to do in order to grow and he replied that he did not. I then asked her to have the animals form a circle with the dove in the center and to ask each animal to shine its love and support on the dove as if it were a beam of light emanating from each animals heart. Dove stood in the center absorbing the light and then began flying in a circle above them, higher and higher, until he was out of sight. A few moments later a large and noble eagle began circling down and landed in their midst. The animals were amazed, but expressed sadness that the dove was gone. The eagle replied that he had all the qualities of the dove plus much more strength and that he would be able to do things that the dove could not, such as catch rabbits for the puppies to eat.

At this one of the puppies asked, "What does rabbit taste like?"

Mary laughed.

Our sixth session took place two weeks later. Mary was depressed. She had been to visit her parents and had become involved in some conflict with her mother. She realized that her mother was still trying to treat her like a child and became upset and manipulative whenever Mary asserted her independence. She was also beginning to remember the pain and loneliness of her long stays in the hospital as a child.

Upon going to meet the animals she saw that the puppies were almost fully grown and that the four were of different breeds: a Bassett hound, a German shephard, a French poodle, and a Redbone hound.

All the animals were doing well except for the fox who was absent. He came when called but his hair was matted and he was extremely thin. It was evident that he was dying. A voice told Mary that the fox must die in order to change but that he would not die unless she allowed it. In great sadness she agreed and they all carried it to its cave where it died. They all mourned, particularly the Bassett hound who had been it's best friend.

At the seventh session the following week I saw that Mary had fixed her hair differently. She was positive, direct, and settled. She said that she had been feeling very good for the past few days but did not know why.

When she visited the animals she saw that a bighorn sheep had joined them in place of the fox. He said that he and the eagle lived very close to each other, and that he and the elephant would work very well together. The elephant agreed that they would.

I had Mary ask the animals when might be an appropriate time to go back and visit the young girl in the hospital to see about healing her injuries. The bighorn sheep replied in a week or two. The others agreed.

The eighth session was held two weeks later and Mary reported that she had been feeling very good since our last session.

In the visualization all the animals were waiting for her. I had her ask them whether this would be the proper time to go back and heal the little girl in the hospital who was suffering from burns on her legs. They all replied positively. I suggested to Mary that the animals would know how to get there.

When they arrived at the hospital Mary was shocked to see how small the girl was, and described her as having a far away look in her eyes.

The girl was surprised to see all the animals. Three of the puppies immediately crawled under the bed. The elephant gave her a doll he had brought her. The eagle stood at the head of the bed and the owl at the foot. The dogs licked her burned legs and then stood her on her feet. As she walked between them she grew stronger.

The dogs had healed her legs when suddenly Jesus arrived to heal her spirit (Mary's words). He picked her up but she kicked and lashed out at him in anger. He calmly carried her to a pool, bathed her, and then brought her back to the animals. Her anger was now gone.

She then rode on the elephants back and returned with them to the glen where the animals lived. Along the way she grew bigger and bigger, and just before they arrived at the glen she and Mary joined together and became one. All the animals rejoiced. There was a beautiful sunset.

When Mary had completed the visualization she was

rosy complexioned and beaming. She said she felt great.

Although our ninth session was scheduled for two weeks later, Mary called me in five days to say that she was feeling forlorn and sad. She said she felt that in some way it involved her relationship with her mother.

I had her come in immediately and we did a visualization to meet her animals. She found them in an open field which was unusual as they had always previously met in the glen. The poodle informed her that there was going to be a lot of emotional pain. When she inquired as to its source the giraffe told her that it involved conflict over acceptance and rejection. When she asked how to deal with it she was told that it must be lived through now because she didn't face it when it originally occurred, and that she needed now to accept it as a vital step in her growth. She was also told that it would not be coming up now if she were not ready to face it. I had her ask if we should do any specific work on it at this time. The animals advised her to just stay in close touch with them and to face whatever came up, but that it was not necessary to do anything specific about it right now.

Mary called me one evening five days later. She said she had been going through an intense bout of feeling lonely and forlorn. I asked her to talk to her animals about it and then call me back.

She called back twenty minutes later and said they had reminded her of a time during her high school years when she and her parents had moved to a small town. The students at the school were very cliquish and had rejected Mary. She was hurt by this and became very much of a loner, escaping into books and never facing the pain. A second event involved a close relative who had suddeny rejected her for no known reason. Mary was now accepting the anguish and loneliness that were involved in both of these situations.

I saw Mary for the last time four days later. She was beaming, exhilarated. She told me she had been for a long drive and had seen many things for the first time even though she had taken the drive many times before. There was an aliveness and a vibrance about her that I had not previously seen. I spontaneously said that this was probably the last time she would have to see me, and she immediately replied that her animals had already told her the same thing.

She said each animal was now in its own new home and although they were still very close, each now lived in its own domain. She felt she was closing a door on a segment of her life and a whole new direction was beginning. She said she felt like everything had been together at one time, then it all fell apart, and now it was back together again. She knew the direction in which she was heading and it was all good although she did not know the specific details.

I asked her to thank her animals for me and she reported back that Hooty, her Communications animal, wanted me to know that although it had been slow, he had grown from being a caricature and was now a live owl three feet tall.

Chapter Seven
Reflections

I want to present here my thoughts about this particular case and though I speak from the perspective of my own metaphoric view it must not be overlooked that each client also has a very personal understanding of the animals. Furthermore we must also keep in mind that even though the imagery is open to metaphoric understanding and interpretation it is much more than that. Each animal is alive. Each animal is in the moment. Each animal is a representation of a deeper functioning quality which itself is related to the other qualities and to the image of the individual him/her-self. Each animal is also a vehicle for enhancing growth, i.e., becoming more attuned to those deeper elements.

The animal can also be an instrument for impeding growth, and this happens when there is a deterioration in the relationship between the individual and the animal. For this reason it is necessary to closely monitor the relationship when therapy is first begun, and to insist that the individual move toward a respect for the animals. It is no more than asking that the individual begin to respect him/her-self. Anything else perpetuates dis-integration and lack of wholeness. This does not mean that the individual need obey the animals, for in some cases they may have an axe to grind when initially encountered, and further reason why the individual needs to get in touch with the council as soon as possible so that detractors from unity can be immediately spotted and worked with. This is frequently initiated by the other animals.

When I speak of "the individual", as in the previous paragraph I am referring to that individual's identity, and the identity is only a part of the totality of who that individual is, for obviously he/she is also ultimately the animals and those functions of which the animals are an appearance, as well as the relationships between the functions, etc. But "the individual" does not recognize this broader, deeper self, and it is the maintenance of an identity separate from, and in many cases opposed to, this larger inclusive being that itself is the crux of the problem.

Mary's first image, the growth of the seed, indicates a sensitive and tender (and perhaps tenuous) connection with the sources of her nurturing. But it is good that the threadlike roots go deep. And the energy available for her growth is rich. She is strong, perhaps a bit thick, or dense, and protective. The flower indicates her sensitivity and balance, and her growth will be full if she will allow it rather than trying to determine it, and if she will see to providing what is necessary for that growth.

The intellect (the fox) has hidden away from attempts to contain it or force it into certain molds. And there is some anger about these attempts. It has also apparently become rather foxy, and one can imagine Mary learning to give teachers what they appear to want and to gear herself toward answering test questions rather than allowing the intellect to grow into its own dimensions, while hiding away the nucleus of her own unique and sometimes oppositional thoughts, a situation that may be true of many students.

This is further evidenced by the fact that she has apparently given more attention to her words (the owl caricature) than to their content, so that her communication is really a poor representation rather than something vitally alive. And her intellect is saddened by this.

The fact that her heart is a dove indicates that she is a

45

peacemaker rather than someone who makes waves, and its initial statement to her (that she needed to know she was not like everyone else, that she was an individual and needed to accept the fact) tells us that she has probably done this by trying to fit herself to a mold rather than accepting her individuality.

Her power (the turtle) is heavily protected or defensed and she is slow to use it. It expresses a great fear of me so I reassure it and let it know that I trust it and will not intrude upon it, for it needs to know that I do respect it in its process. It also informs her that she needs to be more attentive to detail and not get lost in busyness; this type of activity has possibly been one of her main ways of avoiding things she needs to face and deal with. Her power is also closely related to her communication.

But the main place that her growth needs to occur and in fact is incipient, is in her emotions (the puppies). It is this element whose development becomes a process by means of which the integration of all her components occurs. When we first meet Mary her emotions are probably not much more than an introject of her mothers emotions, or of emotions that her mother expected her to have (i.e., the mother dog). But they are quickly beginning to differentiate, entering into a beautiful process of emotional individuation, spurred by a caring for and loving her emotional self.

Her grounding/security is very stable (the splayed legs of the giraffe) and can see far (its long neck). It immediately assumes a leadership role (it is the first to meet her at the fourth session) and it is also the element that initiates the integration and assumes responsibility for seeing that her emotions are properly nurtured and cared for. Her love and communication are given the task of supporting and nurturing her emotions. Her power assumes responsibility for the cleanliness (clarity/ integrity) and freshness of her emotions (in their expression), and the intellect, experiencing a particular connection to one of them, agrees to an awareness of them and their caring/cleaning. So that all of the other abilities move into a relationship with her emotions which is supportive and which fosters their healthy growth. Through her emotions the other qualities are also developing relationships with each other which have a common and cooperative focus.

The curious dream and spontaneous visualization that occurred between the fourth and fifth sessions requires some comment. Mary is in her house (in her being), asleep (unaware) and something entered which didn't belong there (an introjection). She could not identify it nor could she articulate it, but she recognized it through feeling and she immediately took action and chased it out of the house. The fact that the dream was vivid indicates its importance in her life. And her mode of recognition and action is occurring at the intuitive level. There is no vacillation but only a deep trust of her awareness and the correctness of her action.

If we use the dream as an overlay for the spontaneous visualization which she reported next we experience a very comfortable fit, and it feels like the same event is playing itself out at a different level. Mary is with her animals when something foreign arrives, the two swans. The fact that the swans are black and white immediately indicates to me that they probably belong to the level of linguistic polarization, i.e., the tendency of language to classify objects and events into opposing categories. This is frequently indicated at the intellectual and communication levels, but at other levels also, by animals that are black and white: zebras, skunks, etc. My interpretation is further substantiated by the fact that the owl, the communication animal, was accepting of them. The fact that the swans want to build a house for the puppies indicates that their concern is with the creation of a conceptual structure within which the emotions can be contained. Of course this is one of the travesties that is imposed on us by being verbal animals and social beings: we learn at home and particularly in school that the principal way to function is to subordinate experience, and particularly emotional experience, to verbalization, or conceptualization. We are taught not to accept our experience as valid unless we can describe or explain it. This is perhaps one of the social introjects that is most devastating to our individual wholeness. It is exactly this misguided philosophy that Thorndike was expressing when he stated that everything that exists can be measured: the reduction or translation of all experience into concepts, as if *conceptualization* were the foundation rather than *experience;* the static depiction of a dynamic process. In therapy one frequently hears people wanting to "understand" their emotions, or "know what they mean". They assume an identity based on ideas and concepts and "what people may think of them", rather than living the dynamic and passionate feelings that they have.

The fact that none of the other animals are accepting of the two swans indicates that they don't belong there, and Mary trusts her animals enough to take action and reject the introjects.

As they leave they turn into "lizard-like creatures". In my own experience with this work the appearance of lizards or alligators or crocodiles, perhaps reptiles in general, indicates the focus of a rather primitive defense system, or territoriality, at that particular level. Upon rejection we can see the swans perhaps reversing their evolution, returning to the primitive defense (i.e., rejection or acceptance) which is the foundation of a territory, and perhaps also the nucleus of conceptual differentiation. Many lines of thought could be followed from here, including a baby's dirty diaper being among the first occurrences that engender social rejection, and the fact that olfaction was evolutionarily the first sense to be developed.

The question can also be raised hypothetically as to what might have happened had the two swans been allowed to stay. My guess would be that Mary would have found herself trying to explain or account for her developing emotions within the framework of a socially acceptable paradigm, would then experience some of her emotions to be in conflict with some conceptual constraints and would oppose, limit, find fault with, etc., her emergent feelings, rather than letting them grow to their fullness in relation to the rest of her being.

I feel also that the dream and her spontaneous visualization, and within these her awareness, perception, and action, are also closely related to the rapid growth of her power, the explosive growth of her turtle, so that defense was no longer its primary concern. She is willing to trust her perceptions and her deeper being, and to act on these

At the fifth session her heart (dove) indicates that her intellect (fox) needs to grow, but her communication (owl) and grounding (giraffe) systems feel that this should not happen until there has been a bit more emotional development (until the puppies are a bit more grown), and that it is actually time for her heart to grow. Her heart grows in strength and size beyond that of a peacemaker, (although it still contains those qualities) to an element that can *actively* nurture her emergent emotions (an eagle). And that this might further involve Mary facing and digesting her timidity and fear (the rabbits).

By the sixth session we see that Mary's growth is coming into conflict with parental forces that would subordinate it to their own focus. This is not too surprising as most people, in our society at least, have remained emotionally at the level of children. Our social vehicles are geared toward the education and maturation of the intellect but not equally toward the evolution and full growth of the emotions. And control, particularly verbal control, is probably the primary fixation between most people. And we see Mary's mother, probably at this point experiencing Mary's strength in being her own person, straining the limits of her own power to keep Mary subordinate, but in so doing refusing to allow her own growth to proceed beyond its current limits.

Upon looking within we see that the present development of Mary's emotions, and their individuation and differentiation, is almost complete. It is now time for her intellect to grow. She has come to appreciate her intellect and its survival instincts, and feels a warmth and caring for it. There is also a sadness about letting it change. She is informed that she has the capacity to resist its growth and evolution. Her relation to her own growth must be one of *actively allowing* it. What a misunderstanding we typically have of allowing, as if it were a passive event. And we see here with Mary the relationship between clinging and allowing, between freezing ones development and trusting ones growth. We see the vital importance of the attitude that we assume toward ourselves. It was beautiful to watch Mary actively assume responsibiliity for the evolution of her intellect and to accept the emotions that went along with this change.

By the seventh session we see the emergence of her new intellect, the bighorn sheep: sure footed, balanced, agile, capable of scaling heights and climbing peaks rather than its traditional way of hiding itself in a cave. Now it is capable of exposure, and also of quick movement. This is an intellect that is also very close to her heart and that can work in close coordination with her power. And we can sense a new step in the integration of her elements further expressed in her appearance and composure, and her new being feels good to her.

The eighth session represents something that I undertake when necessary: bringing the animals together in the healing of an early trauma. It is always fascinating to watch the animals spontaneously take charge of the healing, knowing exactly where and how the healing needs to occur. And we can see the complexity of the trauma involved. Not only is there the physical injury to the legs, but there is also the emotional trauma of isolation and helplessness, of being small in a world dominated by grownups, and of being angry at ones spiritual fate. The spontaneous appearance of Jesus is interesting, indicating that perhaps as the injured child she had railed at God, or rejected spiritiual consolation, an action which itself needed healing. The girls growth following the healing, and ultimate union with Mary, indicates that the healing was successful. And whether or not any physical problems remain, the psychological, spiritual and emotional dimensions have matured to a point of being consonant with Mary's chronological development.

The next event, Mary's telephone call to me, was significant in several ways. In the first place it indicated that she was attentive to what was occurring within her, listening and trusting, even if she did not understand. Secondly it indicated she felt trusting enough of me to call at a time that was unusual, and to request help.

During the session that followed, the fact that the animals met in a new location (the open field) is significant. The animals meeting in a different location usually foreshadows new dynamics, or a recentering of the individual. Furthermore, the statements the animals make indicate that they have a good overview of the situation, being able to anticipate coming processes in Mary's growth. The poodle, one of her emotional animals, tells her that there will be a lot of emotional pain. The giraffe tells her that it involves conflict over acceptance and rejection, so we get a sense of the grounding animal being attuned to acceptance and rejection, or these elements playing a vital role in the development of her sense of security. Furthermore, we learn that experiences must be lived through (something reminscent, to me, of Krishnamurti's The First and Last Freedom, 1975) if our growing is to continue. And that experiences that have not been "lived through" present themselves to us, or re-present themselves to us, when we are ready for that step in our growth.

The manner in which I as therapist trust the animals in regard to both the content and the pacing of the therapy comes through clearly in this session. Were I involved in some other theoretical orientation at this time, Gestalt therapy, for example, I would undoubtedly have attempted to work with her feelings of sadness and feeling forlorn. Following the guidance of the animals feels much more precise and natural, as if both she and I are being guided from a dimension that knows much more specifically what needs to occur in her growing, which in this case involved doing precisely nothing at the moment. In fact I, as therapist, am *ultimately* dispensable when it comes to her growing. I am essentially the vehicle that gets her from the place of being dependent upon someone else for the acknowledgement of her growth to that place of being independent and trusting and allowing the uniqueness of her own being to evolve at its own pace and into its own dimensions, with the participation of her own awareness.

Her next call is also a good portrayal of my relationship with her. There is no need to do any counselling over the phone. Anyone who has ever tried it knows the frustration and limitations involved. Instead I put her in touch with her own process, a dimension which both of us have learned to trust by now. And this is really a distillation of how I work in a therapy session as well. For example, if the client tells me how they feel about a particular animal I ask them to repeat what they have said to the animal itself. I am not there to have them develop a relationship with me, even though I characteristically come to care for them and am deeply moved by their growth. My task is to help them develop a particular relationship with themselves, one that is nurturing and supportive of their growth and evolution. Their relationship to me or my relationship to them is very secondary to this. And it is good for Mary to recognize that her relationship with her animals is her own, and that her growing in her relationship to them can take place without me. Essentially, I am superfluous at this point.

At our final session I felt Mary's energy as soon as she entered the room. She was radiating a tangible and positive fullness. In working with others I have felt a similar radiant energy at times that a significant integration takes place. In her description of where she had been there was a sparkling openness and aliveness. Our interaction was spontaneous and in the moment. Our first words were quite significant for the question of when does therapy end: it ends when the animals say it has. And therapy also ends when the animals have done their full growing. The last animal to grow was the owl, her communication animal, (interestingly, difficulty in communication being what had brought her to me in the first place). Still in its natural wisdom but now depicted in its magnificently large aliveness.

Her description of herself made me think of the descriptions of the journeys of shamans: through dismemberment and into reconstitution as a new being. And even though our descriptions and understanding of shamans is sketchy, it is told that in some cases they had as many as seven animal helpers (Eliade, 1964). At this session she also gave me permission to write about her as I have.

This was actually not the last time that I saw Mary. I saw her again about a year later. She had just quit her job and was taking some time to explore new directions. Her family and friends were unified in their horror of her quitting a "perfectly good job" for no apparent reason and with no other job to go to immediately. This concerned Mary and made her question whether she had done the right thing. In talking to her animals they all agreed that this was the thing to do and so she ceased to doubt the appropriateness of her actions. Mary had also become part of a religious denomination and was writing music.

In speaking of her animals she told me that one of the puppies had given birth to a litter of three, indicating a continued growth and further differentiation of her emotions.

She also told me that a new animal, a hawk, had spontaneously appeared, and that it seemed to be a part of the group even though it held itself somewhat aloof from them. I took this to be her spiritual animal, an animal that I had not specifically included among the animals at the time that I began working with her.

Chapter Eight
The Crown Animal

During the first year following the discovery of the Personal Totem Pole I worked only with the centers that corresponded to the first six chakras. Classically The first chakra is located at the base of the spine but in my work I had the client focus on feelings located in the pelvis, legs and feet simultaneously. This was done for purposes of decorum in the small, conservative community where I worked. I have since explored using either the pelvis or the base of the spine as the focal point and have found no essential difference. The animal that emanates from this area is called the Grounding animal and its psychological function involves ones relationship with the earth and also ones sense of security, the ground on which one stands.

The second chakra is located in the gut or belly and is related to the emotions and passions. The third is in the solar plexus and is related to the power to act clearly, decisively, and effectively. The fourth is in the heart and is related to love and compassion. The fifth is in the throat and relates to communication, and the sixth is in the forehead and is concerned with the intellect and intuition.

But there is also a seventh chakra, the Crown chakra, situated at the very crown of the head, which had been curiously absent in the totem pole that my client initially observed at her turning point. The Crown chakra is concerned with the relation to one's spirit, and I made no attempt to explore its dynamic role during that first year.

Then in the Summer of 1983 I was contacted by Bill, a

young professional who was specifically interested in undergoing the Personal Totem Pole process. In his early thirties, he was having difficulty relating to his wife and children, being faultfinding and highly critical of them. He was intelligent and articulate, lean and intense, and had recently lost both parents in an automobile accident.

During our first session, as I was conducting him through the process, the animal that emerged from his forehead was a skunk who said to him, "I'm very beautiful. I go along just living my life and if someone bothers me I really let them have it, if someone tries to injure me". When I had Bill ask the skunk if there was anything it needed from him, it replied, "Respect the space that I need for going about my life."

His throat animal was a bear, and he described it in the following manner: "It's ferocious. It's big....I don't know if it's a grizzly bear or just a brown-black bear. Again, it's just going along eating and minding its own business." When he asked the bear if it had anything to tell him, the bear said, "I could destroy you!" This both frightened and saddened Bill, and the bear continued, "You don't see me as I am. Just look. Remember what you saw the first time? Just going along the trail, eating. Respect the space that I need to nourish myself." Bill told the bear that he would not intrude in its space. He then said to me, "the bear says that it will let me know if I do, and it's the ferocity that I'm going to feel if I do that."

When I asked Bill to focus on his heart and allow an animal to emerge from his heart, he said, "What occurred to me immediately is a humming bird, bluish humming bird with a rose-reddish breast"

"I had the image that it had a butterfly in its mouth. There's something ugly about that. I don't know if it's saying to me or what, but it's like "Do you see how frantic this is, destroying beautiful things, flying around like crazy. I need to rest. I need to perch somewhere." The beating of the wings isn't rhythmic. There's something a little bit off about it."

"It says, 'I need you to let go of me so I can just go my way and you can be like yourself. So that you're not like me and I'm not like you. Because you're causing me to fly crazy and do things that aren't in my nature.' What I think is that I don't know what my own heart is like. It just keeps saying, 'Well, be who you are.' It's telling me, 'You're not like me.' It's like a counterfeit image. There's something desperate about this humming bird. I've really impaired it. Almost like seabirds that have oilspill on their wings. It's telling me this isn't the real image. This isn't the real animal. It's almost like 'well, you're not going to know right now. I'll serve as an example of what you're not.'"

I had Bill ask the humming bird if it would be willing to participate as a member of a council of animals, he replied, "It's angry. It's as if it has it's own interest in serving on that council. As a way of freeing itself of me."

I asked Bill to focus his awareness on his solar plexus and allow an animal to emerge. He said, "It's a jungle. It's almost like a Rousseau painting. A lot of beasts. A lot of powerful wild beasts. Gorilla, lions... a mouse. The images of dark, powers, forces. I don't know about the mouse. It seems like the gorilla...has some power there. He says to me something like, 'I'm the symbol that you can most readily understand about this part of yourself.'

"He says, 'You're afraid of your own strength. And you turned me into a mouse. And seeing me as a gorilla shows how afraid you are of me.' I tell him, 'I *am* afraid of you. I turn you into a mouse. Maybe I'm afraid that you could destroy me too.'

And he says, 'If you don't do something about me I will.'

"He says, 'I'm a raging wild animal. And what you need to do is see the way, so that my diffuse, wild energy has a direction to go. Otherwise I'll get so frustrated I'll tear you limb from limb.' It says to me, 'How dare you treat us like this!!' And it's talking for the other animals so far. 'How can you do this to us?' I feel really sad, like I've just been so...like I've wronged them.

"It tells me, 'You'd better pay attention to us now. We can tell you everything you need to know, but you'd better pay attention or we'll kill you.'

"It feels very firm, very angry, and very loving. It would kill me...if it had to. To keep something else going on. To keep its own energy from being destroyed. This is a real strong one. In a way it feels like the leader, the spokesman, for the others so far."

In allowing an animal to emerge from his gut, Bill said, "A pig is what I see first, indulging itself. It says, 'I'm misunderstood. And you people throw all of your worst and lowest opinions onto me. All that I'm doing is living my life. And all kinds of food are acceptable to me. But you see me as slovenly and rolling around in garbage. And what I'm doing is I'm just living my life. What's going on is *you're* rolling around in garbage. The ugliness is *you.* '"

Bill continued, "I want to know how it lives. I want to know how it goes about it's life. What's the difference, and how are we the same? The pig says, 'I accept what comes my way in order to live. And I can accept more than you can.' This makes me feel very sad. I don't feel peaceful. And the pig is so obviously peaceful. And it tells me, 'You see garbage, and slovenliness, and ugliness. I see food, and life. You don't see me as I am. All you see is your ugliness that you throw onto me. Watch me.'

"The pig is so clean. It's spotless. And I keep putting a muddy, dirty, hairy ugliness onto it. It says to me, 'Everything that there is is food to help you grow.'"

I had Bill ask the pig if there was anything it needed. "'No. I can accept anything,' it says, 'whatever is presented to me, I can accept. What I need from you'" it says, 'what I would like from you, but I don't need it, what I would like from you, for your sake, is for you to see me as I am. If you see me as I am, you free yourself.' I want it to be on the council.

"It seems like it will be there, but to listen. It's receptive, it seems. And accepting. And I think it can teach me some things in that way."

When I asked him to focus his awareness on his pelvis, legs, and feet, and to allow an animal to emerge from this area, he said, "The first thing that occurred to me, the only thing, but I feel a lot of resistance about it, is a caterpillar. It's just kind of wiggling around. It's just wiggling around like a penis. It says, 'You don't know what to do with me, and you don't know what to do about me.' Yeah. Sort of like, all I have is the old ways. It says, 'Let go of the past.' I think I am. It says, 'I cannot help but let go of the past', about itself. It says that it's not in it's nature to hang onto the past. It just keeps going. But that I can...I can fight it. It wants me to just watch it, over time, and be with it. Let myself go through in myself what it's going through in itself. 'Don't be what you're not.' is what it's saying to me."

By now I was quite concerned about Bill and his obvious lack of relationship with his animals. The apparent ferociousness and potential destructiveness of the Bear and the gorilla, the franticness and anger of the humming bird, the tendency of the skunk to attack when provoked, the apparent distorted perception about the pig, and the fact of a caterpillar as a grounding animal all caused me concern.

I felt there was a desperate need for something more positive, some aspect of Bill's deeper being with which he might have a more positive relationship, so I decided to try accessing the Crown animal. I asked Bill to allow an animal to appear immediately above his head.

"What comes right away is a unicorn. It's beautiful. It's dazzlingly white and glowing. And its horn is going straight up.

"It said, 'You have no idea how beautiful I am.' And it says that with no ego. It says it with joy and love. Almost like, 'Have you got something in store for you! When you ride me, I take you to God.'"

I had Bill ask if it could take him there now.

"It says now isn't the time. What it says is, 'You need to purify yourself. You need to be ready. You need to let go of some things. You need to be naked. And when you're ready, then we'll go.' It's just really great!

"It says, 'Please do it. Let yourself have it.' It's so beautiful! You have no idea!

"I'm just really drawn toward it. I want to do it. I'll do what I need to do to be with it, to go."

I had Bill ask the unicorn if it would go with him to gather the animals together into a council. He replied, "It's hesitant."

I then had him ask if he should gather them and bring them to the unicorn. He replies, "That's what it is, I should bring the things up to it, and ring them around it. I'll do that."

"There's the skunk. The skunk starts scurrying up. It's so beautiful. And the bear lumbers along. It knows the way. Humming bird flies right up. The gorilla is so great. It's so incredibly powerful. It just goes like Tarzan, from tree to tree and just swings right up. The pig sort of just smiles and just walks slowly toward the circle. And the caterpillar, even before this, was crawling up a branch going up. It goes right across, reaches across space... The unicorn, it's legs are just going. It's like it barely touches the earth because its got so much upward energy. And it's right in the middle. Almost like the tapestry in the cloister in New York, of the unicorn with the fence around it. Except instead of the fence there are all these animals. There's the skunk, the bear. The humming bird is still going, it's not resting. And the gorilla, so monstrous and stern looking. And the pig is just lying there, looking, breathing. The caterpillar...right there, just looking."

I asked Bill to thank them for coming together and to make a statement to them concerning his commitment to growing, and requesting their support and participation.

"They're wary. They're not wary, they're skeptical. And yet they say, 'We have everything you need.' There's a lot of caring. Kind of like...a brotherhood."

I had Bill ask them if they would consult among themselves to see what their first order of business should be.

"I see heads nodding. And they go off. They all kind of gather around....the circle breaks up and they go off and all I see is heads and rear ends and they're talking among themselves. I'm by myself looking at them about 15 feet away. They're huddling. I think they're all saying, 'He's been disregarding me.' 'He's been seeing me all wrong.' 'He hasn't been paying attention to me.' 'He has to get in touch with me.' Some kind of golden light, white light, showers down from the top of the unicorn's horn onto all of them, suggesting, and the words are, 'He has to remember where he's going.' And that light touches all of the animals....as if....that....clarifies the meaning of each one of them in my life. The unicorn and the caterpillar let that light....this is very confusing...

"There's a lot going on. they're all talking, they're all mumbo jumbo, I hear little bits of things. I think what they're going to do is....select a spokesman. Because they're all....you know what it is, they all feel so ignored for so long that they're all just....the unicorn is trying to calm them down, and yet the unicorn isn't a good spokesman because.... he's too.... too removed.... too.... something different about the unicorn. It's almost like.... an ultimate.... phenomenon of some kind. So.... is it the skunk?....It feels like it's the gorilla. One of them says, 'How about if he devotes a day to getting to know each one of us. There's seven of us, seven days in a week, and he could visit one of us each day for the next week.' It seems like there's some interest in this. They feel like.... like they're strangers to me. Not like I'm a stranger to them, they've been watching. But they're strangers to me. It kind of offends them. And they feel a little bit slighted. A lot slighted. Now they're saying, 'Well, all right. What's going to be the easiest thing for him to deal with? Who's going to be the easiest one for him to be with?' And it seems like it's the skunk. So okay.

"I don't know what to do next, and they're just sort of watching, waiting for me to do something."

I asked Bill if he would be willing to do as they suggested, spending some time each day with them, one at a time. He replied affirmatively, and following some dialogue as to the mechanics of these meetings, Bill said, "Even if *I* don't mean business, *they* do. They're going to continue, as they always have, even if it costs me my life. I feel ashamed of how full of insincerity I am. It's like I... I want them to teach me about being clear. And the caterpillar says, 'Watch me. Find that clarity in yourself.' One of them, I don't know which one, and maybe just the caterpillar again, says, 'Be alert for simple things to do, and pay attention while you do them. Do them with your complete attention.' Then an image of the gorilla, saying, 'It's the same, you know, with all of us. We all have different energies and different styles and different things, but we're all expressing ourselves very clearly, very simply.' They're showing me my own mucky stuck-in-thoughtness. It feels done."

I was deeply moved by the power of the unicorn, as was Bill. As soon as it appeared it provided a focus for the other animals, giving them a unified direction; transporting them beyond their initial anger at Bill into a unified concern with his growth. And it also gave him a direction that was positively energized. The step from the first 6 animals to the unicorn in this case exhibited the psychological effect of going from dissension and fragmentation into alliance and integration. Although much growth had been effected in previous clients by working only with the first 6 chakra animals, I saw the Crown animal's potential for cutting through apparent problems and moving to a new level of unified functioning. From this day on I began including the Crown animal in the Personal Totem Pole process.

My own Crown animal had been seemingly absent in the totem pole seen by the client who first led me into this work, and so my initial explorations had omitted this also. Later, in seeking my own Crown animal, I became aware of the possible reason it was not initially observed: it was not an animal but a shaft of golden sunlight.

Chapter Nine
Nobody Will Ever Talk to Me Again

In early 1984 a woman came to see me who had heard one of my talks on guided imagery. She told me that she had been an alcoholic for most of her life and had been through numerous programs and therapies in attempts to deal with it. She was currently a member of Alcoholics Anonymous and had been a "dry alcoholic" for the past seven years. She was 39, ran her own business and attended some evening classes, and had recently left a relationship of several years duration. She was thin, tense and there was a sense of something brittle about her. Her name was Sue.

I instinctively began my guided imagery with Sue at a place that I had explored with only half a dozen people at that time: with the hand animals. I had first begun to explore the technique of allowing an animal to emerge from each hand in an attempt to see if this could be used for assessing imbalances between the left and right cerebral hemispheres and for working toward an integration between them.

The animal that emerged from Sue's left hand was a little black Scotty dog in a cage in a pet shop. It said it wanted a home and needed to be loved and taken care of. She told it she would give it a home but it was afraid to go home with her, afraid of the big German Shepherd.

"I told the Scotty dog I'd protect it but it's still scared," Sue said. "It has no way to protect itself from this big dog. It would try to be friends if I would be there anytime the big dog is with it. It's happy now, licking me and snuggling all over."

I then asked Sue to allow an animal to emerge from her right hand. It was the big German Shepherd, angry and snarling.

"It's angry that I would bring something home for it to share. It doesn't want to share and it's telling me it'll hurt this little dog if I ever let him down. He says he's been running the house and in charge of it and he's not going to share. I try to pet him and he's growling at me, pacing back and forth and staring at me. I'm afraid to take the little dog out from under my coat. He might attack me as well as the little dog. And at this moment I don't know whether I can put him outside, because if he doesn't want to go I couldn't put him out. He's not happy.

"He has the body of a Shepherd but the face of one of those African dogs. It's like his face is too small for his body. I asked him about it and he says 'I'm half wild, half tame.' He's unpredictable and hard to manage. Sometimes the wildness in him overtakes his tameness. He wants to be tame like other dogs, but yet a side of him is vicious and shows no mercy to his prey."

I asked Sue "What is his job with you?"

She answered,"To keep me alive."

I continued, "Is this the job of the head or of the body?"

"It's the job of the head."

"What's the body's job?"

"To be my companion and to protect me."

"Isn't this sometimes a conflict?"

"He doesn't know about conflict."

I asked her to tell him that he's just one of a family of animals and that she'll be getting them all together soon.

She replied, "He doesn't want to meet them."

"Why not?"

"Because he's only concerned about himself and his survival."

I asked her to tell him that she is also concerned about his survival, that she does need him to protect her, but that right now she's also concerned about growing.

"He really doesn't trust me. He only trusts himself. And when he's in danger he can puff himself up and make himself bigger. As I talk to him he seems to be growing. Like he has to be bigger than me — no, it's not bigger than me, it's bigger than anybody he might meet."

"Isn't this kind of a strain sometimes?"

"He doesn't know about that. All he says is he knows how to do whatever he needs to do to control, to be tough, to be most important."

I asked her to tell him she's happy to be getting to know him, and to acknowledge that she has neglected him for some time, and then to leave.

Because of the intense discrepancy between the two hand animals, and the hostility on the part of the German Shepherd, I made no attempt to bring about any further interaction between them. Frankly, I was concerned, and so I turned to the Chakra animals.

When I asked her to allow an animal to emerge from her forehead she said, "It's like things want to come out but they won't. All I can tell is that it's a bird. It just won't come out. I think it must be frightened."

I asked her to ask it if there's anything it needs from her and she replied, "It's frightened of the big dog."

I then asked her to tell it that she'll be getting in touch with the other animals and will then return.

When I asked her to allow an animal to come out of her throat she replied, "It's a big bullfrog but it won't come out either. It's also afraid of the dog. One bite and he would be gone."

I had her ask what it needs from her.

"Protection! I tell him that I'm willing to protect him. He says he'll believe that when he sees it."

When I asked her to allow an animal to emerge from her heart, she replied in surprise, "It's the little Scotty dog!"

"What's he doing in your heart?"

"He says he's always been there, but he's not young, he's old," Sue replied as she began to cry.

"Ask him if he knows the dog in your left hand."

"He says he's the same. He feels like he's been a baby forever."

"See if there's anything else he needs to tell you at this time."

"It's been a long time since he started trying to talk to me. He's wanted to do so many things and hasn't been able to. Till he thought finally he would be suffocated and die!"

Our therapy hour was over and another client was waiting, but I felt a need to bring Sue into contact with her Crown animal before she left. I asked her to allow an animal to appear immediately above her head.

She replied, "It's a vulture. Almost like he's perched in my head. He's been waiting for the little dog to die."

"How long has he been waiting?"

"For a long time."

I had her ask him if there is anything he needs from her.

"No. I feel he's not going to stay there. Like he's only temporary. He's taking someone else's place. He says that's true. There used to be someone else perched there and he won them away in a battle. This other thing was protecting the little dog, and he finally won him over, so he went away."

"Who was that?"

"He said it was Jonathan the Seagull, and he says that he's the one in my brain. He hides there now. He loves to fly, but he only comes out when he knows it's safe, when the dog and vulture aren't there anymore, or when they're not a threat, or when they're busy, he comes out and glides on the air."

As Sue left the session I asked her to call me if it was at all necessary.

When Sue returned a week later she told me that she had felt fuzzy for a couple of days after our last session. She said she seemed to be on the edge of some old sadness, possibly related to her father.

She then began to tell me that at the age of four she had been molested by some man near her home, although not seriously. The man had been caught and apparently jailed.

After a brief relaxation I asked her to allow an animal to emerge from her solar plexus.

"It's a black bear, just walking around in a clearing in the forest."

"Ask the black bear if there's anything it needs to tell you."

"It says that it really doesn't know me."

"Ask it if there's anything it needs from you."

"It says it needs peacefulness and calmness."

"How can this be achieved?"

"It says by getting my emotions under control. I tell him I'm doing that, and he says, sarcastically, 'Yeah, I've heard that before.'"

I then asked her to allow an animal to emerge from her gut.

"It's a crocodile sitting in the water."

"Is there anything it needs to tell you?"

"No."

"Is there anything it needs from you?"

"To be taken care of better."

"How can this be achieved?"

"By not being so anxious, and by taking better care of myself. Fear makes me anxious."

Sue's grounding animal was a giraffe who was running. I asked her to see if there was anything the giraffe had to tell her?

"He doesn't have much time to talk because he's running from all these things that are chasing him."

"How can you help?"

"By stopping these things that are chasing him."

"What is it that's chasing him?"

"I don't know."

At this point in therapy I introduced a process that I had been using for some time in the Personal Totem Pole work: that of *becoming* the animals.

At the beginning of this work some clients had occasionally experienced themselves as spontaneously aware from the subjective or experiential perspective of the animal. This appeared to lead to remarkable insights, not only in terms of the person themselves but also into the lives of the animals. For example, one person after experienceing herself as her head eagle, flying and then landing on a ledge said to me, "The earth is soft to birds, they don't see rocks as hard, the way we do." Another, after being an elephant, told me that the trunk was so sensitive and delicate in it's movement that it seemed to balance out the solidity and power of the body. Also, that the trunk appeared to be a direct extension of the elephant's brain.

As in all of my work with the animals, they are always given appropriate respect. Becoming the animal is never deliberately undertaken without the consent of the animal in question, and the client also has to feel okay about it as well. The client is then asked to merge into the animal, and to experience him/herself as taking on it's size and shape, it's form and structure; feeling the world through it's skin (or fur, or feathers), seeing through it's eyes, hearing through it's ears, feeling it's emotions, being aware of its orientation and attitude, and of what the world is like for that animal. I then ask the client to tell me what most stands out to them about the experience. When the experience is over the client is asked to emerge fully from the animal and to thank it for allowing the merging.

In this part of the process I always begin with the Grounding animal and move sequentially up toward the Crown animal. This is done for theoretical reasons: to move the Kundalini energy upward. It also allows one to end with the Crown animal which then sets the scene for forming the Council, as I characteristically consult the Crown animal as to the appropriateness and procedure for forming the Council.

When Sue became the giraffe (Grounding animal) she told me "When it runs it has powerful front legs which pull the back part of the body along. The front part of the body is strongest. It's kind of 'schizy', always looking around. It seems to be threatened, like something will jump out at it. It's very jumpy at any little movement. It doesn't know much of anything but fear."

When she became the crocodile (Emotional animal) she said, " It is very slow paced, searching around for something that might fall in the water for a snack or dinner. It's very alert to everything that's going on around it even though it looks kind of dead. Even though it's sensitive, it won't allow itself to feel that. It just glides sleek and smooth in the water and even though it looks cumbersome it's smooth and easy. Like it's waiting for something. I have a feeling that at one time it was in a lot of turmoil and now it won't allow itself to get into that space and feel it."

When she became the black bear (Power animal) she said, "As he walks he kind of just wobbles back and forth. He's kind of in his own space, in his own world, not affected by much around him. He likes to play and sleep and eat and investigate. He doesn't really have too many fears. A fear of being trapped or cornered, like by not being able to get out of a fire, or people cornering him, maybe having to fight. It would fight if it had to but it would rather avoid these things. A feeling of security and surety: 'I know where I'm at. Don't get into my space' kind of thing. A lot of fun."

When she became the Scotty dog she said, "It's like I'm falling from space, going around in circles in a dark, conelike tunnel. There's a lot of fear. It's almost like I won't stop falling. I'm falling and falling, going around in circles in this dark — it's almost like maybe a time tunnel. Now it's a little girl falling, maybe 4 or 5. Maybe it's me. It's got pigtails. I don't remember wearing pigtails. She's hurting and nobody understands. She thinks she's been bad and she doesn't understand why everybody whispers and won't answer her questions. People taking her to the doctor and everybody's so angry. Nobody'll tell her what's going on. She feels that if nobody talks about it she must've done something really bad. She has bad dreams and she goes and sleeps with her mom and dad but still nobody talks to her about her dreams. Everybody seems to want to wrap her in.... in cotton, and she just wants to be free and feel.

"The Scotty dog is back. He's telling me that it's okay, that they didn't understand, they didn't have words to talk to her, and that he's tried to tell me that I'm okay, that I didn't do anything wrong. I feel a sense of taking the responsibility of too many things, of too much blame. The little Scotty dog is tired."

We left the little girl with the Scotty dog and moved on to the Throat animal, the bullfrog.

When she became the bullfrog she said: "He's afraid to speak his mind, really unsure. He would rather hide, rather not come out. Maybe at night when nobody can see. He has a feeling of "why try." He's really a loner."

As the seagull she said: "It's very peaceful to glide. He's very keen and watchful, very good at vision. He wants to soar to so many things. I feel that it's tried times of flying and soaring and that it's gotten hurt and then hides, and then it comes out to try again. It seems to be intelligent, proud. It fears crashing and being locked inside my head."

"Is it locked there now?" I asked.

"Not right now but it has been."

At this point our time was up but before we ended I wanted Sue to go back to see how the four year old girl was getting along. The girl had many questions which Sue answered. Sue told her that her parents had not been angry at her but concerned for her. She told her that her parents had been upset at the man that molested her, but not at her. She told the girl that her parents had a difficult time talking about anything that involved sex and that's why they were so silent. The girl began to relax as she understood more and was now feeling better.

Sue said, "She's wanted someone to talk to for a long time. I love her."

Chapter Ten
Growing Up

When I next saw Sue she told me that she felt confused for two days following our last session. She said also that she had felt the presence of the little girl almost continuously. This frightened her as she didn't know what else might be in there.

But Sue was now more relaxed. She said there was a new calmness in her relationship with her father even though she hadn't told him any of this.

In her visualization the Scotty dog (Heart animal) came spontaneously to meet her. "He's very alert today. He feels good, not sad today."

When asked if there's anything he needs, he replied that he needs for Sue to keep searching for her pain so she'll continue to feel better. She agrees to.

At the suggestion of the Scotty dog they visit the little girl.

"She dosn't look as sad today, she's been playing with the little dog. In fact the little dog and her are very close. She just needs to be close today. She looks forward to my visits. She's waited a long time for someone to comfort her. She seems to have grown. She is older. Around 6. She's very uncomfortable about going to school. Her big brother puts her on the bus and she's kicking. She's always alone. She feels alone because she's always afraid. Afraid of people. Afraid of being away from the house. Maybe it's because nobody told her that bad things aren't always going to happen.

"She's confused. When her mother sees her touching her body she tells her it's not okay, that she shouldn't be aware of her body. Her fear of not being close to people is a fear of doing something wrong. She seems more comfortable after I talk to her. She wants to go away and play. She's trying to play with other kids and finding out it's fun. She's coming back to tell me that she's having fun and thanking me for telling her it's okay. And she wants to explore more of this playing and having fun.

"Seagull (Intellect) is sitting on a ridge looking at us. Seagull has always seemed so afraid, but he's not afraid of the Scotty dog, in fact they'd like to be friends. It's because they've been barred from one another that they haven't been able to be friends. Seagull doesn't want to stay very long and talk because he feels free today and he wants to fly.

"I take Scotty back. He doesn't want me to leave him. It's like he wants to be with me wherever I go. In fact he wants me to be even closer, he wants me to carry him.

"We're just walking along and I'm holding him under my arm. I'm getting flashes of some of the animals. I don't know where we're going. It's like flashbacks of what we've done before.

"I keep seeing a lion. It's like a test to be not afraid to walk over to it and past it. And then when you get there you find out it's not so angry, it's not so big.

"In fact the lion has changed into the big dog. He's still not too happy, but I don't have the sense he's going to bite off the little dog's head. His face keeps trying to change from the wild dog's face to that of a German Shepherd, but it can't.

"The Scotty dog said to him, 'You have to have a heart.'

"He doesn't like that too much because he thinks he does have a heart. I think I must learn more things before I can help him. I feel nervous and anxious like I want to get out of there and I don't know how to get away."

"Tell this to Scotty," I say.

"He says there are the parts of me that I don't understand, that come out when I don't want them to. He says I need to learn more. He'll try to guide me into that learning. I just need to know me and to understand.

"I feel the Scotty dog wants to guide me to my other animals. For some reason I need to hear some things from them.

"We go to see the alligator (Emotions). He says that he can make me hurt physically when I'm hard on myself. That's why he has such sharp teeth and quick actions, but that he would just as soon be peaceful. But if I choose, he can be very angry.

"I feel like the Scotty dog's asking me if I understand. I tell him I do. Scotty dog's telling me I'll learn to not be hard on myself. He says he just wants me to know that when I hurt real bad sometimes that I do have a part of me that can attack me."

They both then left the alligator and our time was up.

When I next saw Sue, a week later, she told me that upon leaving the office the previous week the Scotty dog was very present and when she reached the parking lot it told her it still needed to take her to one more animal. Sitting in her car in the parking lot, Scotty dog took her to see the bear (Power).

Bear was up on its hind legs, roaring. It told her that she doesn't listen to it, that it tells her things and she doesn't listen. It tries to keep her from going in directions that would be harmful or painful but she doesn't listen. She told it she would try to listen more in the future.

Sue also told me that for the past week she has been happy. She has made decisions easily: to go back into Real

Estate, to remain at her parents house for the time being until things are more settled in her own life.

In our visualization Scotty dog is waiting for her. He is full of energy. He's very excited about her taking better care of herself.

"He's also very excited about the fact that I'm thinking of myself and about what might be important to me. And he doesn't feel so bogged down, suffocated, or alone. He says things have been going on since our last visit. He's been visiting. He doesn't feel like he's caged anymore. He's been free to go where he wants and to do as he chooses. He has no gray hairs anymore. He feels closer to me. He has played with the little girl and she feels closer to me.

"I feel a strong pull toward the bear, like the Scotty dog wants me to go see him, so we do.

"The bear just sat down, as if he's going to take time to talk to us. He feels good that I'm listening to him better. And he wants me to know that I'm not always going to listen. But he feels that we're not strangers anymore.

"He's been hibernating through the winter and has just recently come out and he's anxious to help me understand him and to know when he's signalling me.

"He doesn't seem sarcastic today, just concerned, a side of him I hadn't seen. He said one thing, he never gives up, that he will always give me the signals whether I listen or not, that he's not like some of the animals, he doesn't quit or stick his head in the sand.

"He and Scotty dog seem to be closer too. They feel I should visit the other animals. Scotty will go with me. Bear feels very strongly that he really doesn't need any of the other animals; they need to understand his messages and his power. Like he really doesn't want to waste time with them until they're ready to listen to him.

"Scotty and I go to the crocodile. He seems very excited to come up on the bank. He's had a good time swimming around and not having to feel like he's watching or preying on something. He's been enjoying the sun and the water and the peacefulness in his pond. And he doesn't want to take much time to talk. He's sliding back into the water.

"The seagull has come to visit us. He's also had a good time flying around. He hasn't felt caged. He's come in contact with the bear. The bear suggested he think about things he hasn't thought about in a long time. And he's been trying his wings. He's been caged for so long that he's trying to get his bearings. He's even been flying at night, afraid that it wouldn't last. He feels as if there's many things he wants to know and do. But for now he's going to enjoy some space that he hasn't had. He still feels alone, but it's because he's been too involved in making up some time. He's flying off.

"Scotty dog and I are walking along the Crocodile's pond. It's interesting that the big bullfrog is there. He's sitting alongside the pond. He's sunning himself. He just doesn't feel like hiding. He feels like getting some sun and he's really not concerned with "why". He's just going to enjoy. He's not going too far from the edge.

"Scotty dog wants to go see the little girl.

"We're with her. She looks much happier and she's grown. She must be 8 or 9. She's been trying to play with friends. It's very difficult for her. She has a fear of being hurt, of not getting close, of not understanding.

"For the first time she has made herself play with the other kids. She always watched them rather than playing. She gets one friend and she gets too close and then she gets hurt.

"She's not as full of fear now as she was, at least she doesn't feel as if everybody's bad, or going to hurt her. Now she wants to try. Before she couldn't try.

"She's very investigative, wants to take things apart to see what makes them work. This gets her into trouble. She always wants to know why, things there's no answer to or people don't want to tell her.

"She seems not as confused. It's what makes her different. I told her that maybe people don't answer because they truly don't know the answer. Maybe sometimes her mind reaches beyond the people she asks. That's not wrong.

"They're going to test her."

"Who?" I asked.

"The school."

"How does she feel about this?"

"It makes her feel different, scary different. All of a sudden they might take her and put her in another room, even with kids older than her. This is scary to her.

"She's more comfortable knowing I'm with her. She feels like she won't be alone. I told her I fear tests, too."

"Perhaps you can help each other grow beyond this fear of tests," I said.

"She feels good that we can work on that together, that we won't feel alone. I feel she wants me to come visit her more. Especially when I feel uncomfortable, like something's missing. She'll try to tell me when she needs me to come. She says she feels much better, but she feels very alone a lot. And there are so many things that she doesn't understand that when we do talk I help. And she doesn't feel like a bad girl all the time. I feel a lot of comfort being with the little girl. It's like she climbs inside of me and I climb inside of her. It's time for her to go and try to play with her friends.

"The Scotty dog and I are just walking. I don't know if he's saying it or if it's just a thought in my mind, something about the little girl and my soul. He says "the search for your identity is the search for your soul." I feel really comfortable being with the Scotty dog. And he likes being with me.

"He said he became so worried. He thought I was dying and in turn he was dying, he was losing his strength, and that we're best friends because we're getting well together.

"He doesn't have anyplace else for us to go today."

When the session was over Sue told me that she remembered having been tested in the middle of the third grade and she was then moved into the fourth grade where she felt alone, isolated, and incompetent. Since then she has blocked on tests, almost like she sets herself up to fail.

At our next session, she again meets with the Scotty dog and they take a walk to see what they run into.

"Here's the bear, on his hind legs, walking around, like you'd imagine a big ape in a jungle. He feels he's had no conflict in where he's wanting to go. He wants me to realize how powerful he can be, almost like a child boasting about something. I like the bear, he's a neat bear. He's glad we've become friends because he's tried so many times to give his power to me but I couldn't or wouldn't take it. He's encouraged to see that I can use some of his power. He said it's always like there had been something missing. He's saying that he felt for so long that he didn't need anybody, maybe he's been wrong about that. He doesn't seem to have anything more to say, or maybe he wants us to follow him.

"Something's happened to Scotty dog. When I first met him he was so frightened of the big dog. Now he seems to be unafraid.

"The bear has taken us to a den. There's three babies in the den. I feel an anxiety coming over me."

"Tell the bear how you feel," I suggested.

"He says he knows but it's something I must do. One of the babies is dead. He's taken me here to make me realize that Richard was really real. These bears are my sons. Richard died before I could ever see him. And when I came home from the hospital all his things were gone. It's like I had never been pregnant. They had him cremated. All I could do was go to a crematorium and look at a label on a square piece of marble."

Sue weeps.

"The bear's handing me the dead bear and telling me it's okay. Of the other two bears one is strong and one is weak, and the weak one is Thomas and the strong one is Bobby. And I had to make a choice whether I could raise one successfully or raise two and not be able to do anything for them, because Tom was so ill. And the bear's telling me that I shouldn't feel guilty, that I wasn't to blame any more than I was for Richard, but that I should be thankful that his father could take care of him. Bear is telling me not to feel bad about how much I love Bobby, not to let people bring our relationship down, that I love him for three. And that he needed me as much as I needed him.

"The bear said one of his cubs is going to go to someone who doesn't have one and she'll only be left with one. All this time I've thought she was a male. And that she's going to love it as if it were three. She's going to take back that little dead bear out of my arms and she wants me to go with her to bury it. I feel calmer now.

"I didn't know how tightly I had locked these things away."

When the visualization was over Sue spoke to me about her children. Bobby was born when she was only 16. A year and a half later, in her second marriage, she had Thomas.

He was brain damaged and had cerebral palsy. She gave him to his father. The bear made her aware for the first time of "how good that his father could take him."

With Richard her placenta had grown to the uterus, and in addition he was an Rh negative baby. Sue almost died. She remembers hearing the nurse exclaim, "My God, he's deformed!" She never saw him, only heard him cry. She was rushed to surgery. Baby Richard died while she was in surgery. Her parents and husband decided to have him cremated without consulting her. When she came home Richard's room had been made into a family room. She thought it was a bad dream. She didn't know he had been cremated. Her husband said, "Do you want to go see Richard?" Then he took her to a place where there was a plaque on some pink marble.

At the beginning of our next session Sue expressed her views of how imagery could be used in Alcoholics Anonymous. She also said that she is no longer getting embroiled in problems. Now she thinks them through with her whole being.

In the visualization she again meets Scotty dog. He is standing in a forest of big trees. Rays of sunshine are coming down. It's warm. He says the animals are waiting in a clearing not far from here.

"A leopard comes out of the forest to meet us. He's sleek and soft and smooth and friendly. He's our guide for the rest of the way. I feel like I know this animal. He says he used to be the big dog. He says he's finally one thing. He's soft and smooth and has no anger. He's friendly with Scotty dog.

"We're coming to a clearing. All the other animals are there and I greet them one by one.

"The alligator says it's nice to be out of the pond and not feel like he *has* to be there.

"Black bear is sleek and shiny, and glad that I've come this far so that we can all be together. She's glad that I've grown to allow her power to extend to the leopard. I really don't know what she means by that."

"Tell her that you don't know what she means by it," I suggest.

"She said that her and the leopard are very powerful together but they've never been allowed to be together, so only her power has emerged, and that the leopard is a power that I've never known, inner power. She is my strength of letting me know signs of dangers and choices. The leopard is a power of the swiftness of the choices I make, which I've never known. She says as I grow I'll become familiar with the leopard, I'll begin to understand better.

"Seagull says it's time that we use our intelligence. We've had intelligence but our creativity and our flow of where it should go has been covered up by all these strange goings on inside me. He's gathered his strength and he's not weak anymore, and soon we'll explore some things of where we need to go.

"Bullfrog says we don't have to fear saying what we feel. Saying what you feel doesn't mean the other person's wrong and you're right. It's the safety of being able to say where you're at. I need to practice this and not worry about the feelings of others. Worry first about my own feelings.

"Scotty dog has jumped up in my lap. He says to me that he's a part of each one of these animals, but it had gotten so he didn't know any of them. Each one has a tender heart.

"Now that I'm more aware of other things and not just that I'm hurting if I try hard I'll know what needs to be done before it comes to hurting. When it gets to that point it takes a long time to back out just to find where you're at. I must stay in tune with my feelings but I must also stay in touch with Black Bear's signals and Leopard's cunningness to tell me what's to be done quickly.

"Giraffe's coming in. Looking around. Nibbling on trees. He's not shaking and he's — she says first of all that she's a she and not a he. She says since she's been using her senses of smell and her keen sight she hasn't had to worry so much of someone killing her. Rather than be frightened of the times she can enjoy them. Her stature is tall and straight, and I see a strength in her now.

"Scotty dog says he'd like to continue now since the giraffe is here.

"He's only frightened of one thing: that I must learn how to stay in contact with them. That they work well together, it's me that doesn't work with them. I separate them. That they're all gaining a lot of strength that could be stifled again if there's not caution.

"Someday soon, the Scotty dog said, I won't have a guide to go inside me. I must be my own guide. I must try for my own survival. The animals feel that several times a week I should be in contact with them. Even if I'm only in contact with one. That that is my journey for now but I must learn that."

"Can he help you learn that?" I asked.

"It's a journey in learning how to step inside yourself that I must learn for survival. It's not something that can be taught. It's something that either happens or doesn't happen. He has no suggestions other than just try."

When the visualization ended Sue said, "Some of the feelings I have are inexpressible in words. I would like to tell people what's happening with me but there's no way I can, they wouldn't understand. It's so beautiful to find myself feeling differently in situations."

Chapter Eleven
King Cobra

Sue told me she had always been afraid of speaking before a group. Last week, however, she got up and joked and was totally comfortable during a talk she had to give. It was only when she sat down again that she realized how difficult this had previously been. The instructor later remarked to her: "Where is that meek quiet girl that was in my class last year who I couldn't get to say a word?"

Sue also told me that previously she would get totally embroiled in whatever problems would arise in her life, and that now more and more she finds herself concentrating on solutions rather than on problems. This was new to her.

In her visualization she finds Scotty dog standing in the forest. "Leopard has come and joined us right away. He lays down on the grass beside us. And the black bear has joined us. Scotty dog says we need to talk about the week.

"Black Bear tells me how he sent me all kinds of signals this weekend and how for the first time I've listened to his signals and let the leopard react on them. Scotty dog says this is one of the first times that I've felt pain in my heart and been able to find out why and then do something about it. Scotty dog says I feel pain and the bear tells me the signs and the Leopard tells me how to solve it. Scotty dog says that I must consciously work on being aware of another person's pain but not allow this pain to change my reactions of where I must go with it. I must search first for my own feelings. Everyone must have the responsibility of their own feelings.

"The Leopard is telling me that I'm having a lot of stress and I'm still holding onto a lot. And that I shouldn't worry too much about it because it's not something I'm used to using yet.

"I ask Scotty dog why I wasn't able to contact him after Sunday. He's telling me I was dealing with so much and doing such a good job with it that I didn't need further direction and I really did need rest. And that I must learn that contact can come differently at different times. Being aware is contact. Closeness is being in contact, and if I worry about it too much I'll lose contact of the simplest kind, that I'm searching for something I already have.

"Leopard is explaining to me how some of the things I'm feeling that are so different is him; he's not been allowed to do anything before, and that's why sometimes I'll be surprised when I'm asked to do something when I get a signal and I follow through with it. I'm open to him to do it.

"Leopard says that I know it's not what I am or who I'm with, but it's how I perceive myself. Who I really am has nothing to do with who I'm with or what I'm doing, and as I grow this will become more clear to me. That I am good and I'll soon know this myself.

"I can feel Bobby's pain in his situation. Bobby is coming up here the first of the week. I should spend quiet time with him and help draw some of the pain from him, I've been like a good friend but not like a good mother. He's needed that. You can always find a good friend but you can't always have a loving mother.

"I'm leaning against my leopard. Soft fur. I love these three animals very much. I feel so close to the leopard, yet I've only just met him. It's very important that the four of us stay in close contact and that I don't try to rush myself into being all better too fast. Growth comes in stages, sometimes daily and sometimes there are long stretches in between.

"I need to nurture myself. I need to care for myself,

give myself warm fuzzies. Don't be controlled by feelings or emotions or the feelings and emotions of others or you lose your value of decision. Leopard is telling me I must learn to step into these feelings as if it wasn't my own feeling and be able to ask these feelings "Why are you here?"

"Now Scotty dog has jumped up in my lap. He says it's important now that I grasp what I'm learning, and slow down, because I've learned so much, and not to question but just to learn and use what I've known, been taught, what I feel.

"Bear is very happy that when she sends me a signal now at least she feels my alertness of it. I don't run around in a panic, at least not as much of one any more. And the more I use this the more skillful I'll get in just knowing automatically what to do.

"Be aware of my calmness. Being aware of my calmness is when I'm in touch. I need to slow down and start learning how to really use these tools. Bear says I have them, now I must fine tune them.

"I ask Scotty dog why I haven't seen the little girl. Scotty dog replies, 'She's not very little anymore', and the reason I haven't seen her is I've been unconsciously nurturing her. As I stumble across things today that hurt and fix them I'm automatically stimulating her growth to things in the past. That little girl was the same one that dealt with the children. I had the idea that I have all of these hangups and maybe I don't have all these snags, but the snags I've had were really detrimental. That I really haven't dealt badly with *everything* in my life.

"I think that's all they have today."

The next session began with Sue telling me that she had a very trying week. Her granddaughter was ill and emotionally strained, her son was here, a hearing had been held concerning the final termination of the family business. People from Alcoholics Anonymous had been calling her for personal counselling. And she had also been looking at education programs in counseling.

In her visualization she finds the giraffe grazing. He goes with her to meet the other animals.

"Black Bear is walking down a path on her hind legs, then on all fours. She wants me to know that you can walk upright with strength but there's no shame in coming down. I tell her I'm tired. She says I can rest on her for awhile, and she'll help me regain my strength. I walked over to a sunny place. I'm leaning against her thick, soft fur. My body begins to feel very warm.

"Leopard has come out and joined us. Scotty dog is coming up the path. Scotty dog's in my lap. I ask him why didn't I meet with him first. He's really excited, licking me on the side of the face. I want to know why he's excited. He's telling me that I've learned how to walk alone, that I don't always need him to make a journey. He says he's very tired. My heart is very tired, but he's not as tired as usual. All the animals have taken part of the pain and the journey, and he wasn't allowed to take it all.

"Leopard is putting his paw on my legs, saying since I've been allowing him some swift actions that Scotty dog doesn't have to be worn out and Bear doesn't have to become frustrated, and Giraffe doesn't have to feel like running away. I look at Giraffe grazing and resting, her muscles aren't trembling, she's very peaceful.

"Leopard wants to take me back to Tuesday in the courtroom. He wants me to feel what I felt. I felt sadness for my parents that they couldn't feel calmness. How did I feel? I felt relaxed and calm. My heart wasn't beating out of my body and my breath was under control. I didn't feel like I might throw up or faint, or need someone to hold me up.

"Leopard is saying that I'm tired but I'm not crazy with emotion. That I've handled myself well. How did Bobby feel? He seemed fairly calm, as if he'd accepted finally that it was over. He was anxious for it to be over. What do I think of Bobby? I'm proud of him and I was able to tell him that and why. I told him many things I've wanted to, that mainly I'm proud of him and he's strong, and he has every reason to be nuts for what he's been through. He looks good.

"Bear's asking me my feelings for my granddaughter. I feel so close with her. I feel her trials have been so far like mine. Sometimes I wish I could reach in her head and take all her pain away. We have electricity between us. It's almost like I am her or she is me. I know now that she loves her stepmom very much and that she's going to be okay. They're asking me what I learned. I've learned that no matter who it is I want it to be perfect for her. But I've accepted that she has the best she could.

"It was a good experience. This whole week has been one experience after another.

"Leopard is proud of me. He says that when Paul called I was able to see through his conversation. My vision is getting clearer to game players. I've no time for them. My vision has gotten clearer. I would get trapped into things because I wanted to say yes.

"I'm giving my leopard a big hug. I can act swiftly now. I don't have to make dumb mistakes.

"Seagull is flying overhead circling around and around, doing acrobatics. I feel all of the stresses like a wave going over me, like they're being lifted or healed. Scotty dog is curled up in my lap asleep. And I feel almost asleep against the bear. And warm. I feel safe. I feel like a small child curled up in her mother's arms.

"Leopard said before I leave them he wants me to be aware of one thing: to not block out my energy when I'm talking to someone I'm irritated with. To be aware of my own feelings.

"They're telling me it's time to go now. I see them very differently than I saw them three months ago.

At our next session Sue began by talking to me seriously about working toward a degree in counseling. She was looking into various programs.

She also began to talk about her parents, about her mother always seeming to be the brunt of anger at home, and of her father's anger.

So I elected to do some visualization work with her parents. This is work I have done with others which frequently helps dissolve difficulties in relationships by broadening one's view of the situation. I have the client visualize themselves with the person with whom the conflict or lack of understanding is occurring, and then ask them to merge into the person (similar to becoming the animals), so that they gain the advantage of experiencing the complexity of the other's perspective.

She's with her mother in the kitchen, they are sitting at the bar across from each other. Upon becoming her mother she sees her mothers sensitivity and hurt.

In visualizing her father she sees him sitting on a riverbank and feels a wall between them. She can't get through it. She says the wall is made of brick and a shadow.

What is the shadow?

Disappointment.

What event led to disappointment?

The lie she told Dad when she married Gary when she was sixteen: that she *had* to get married. She only told him that in order to get away from home, away from a constantly criticizing grandmother. Then father became very criticizing. He offered no guidance, only criticism. Sue always felt she had to be better than her brother.

I ask her to see if some of the animals would be willing to help heal and resolve the situation. Bear, Leopard, and Scotty dog respond.

Bear says the reason she feels the wall so strongly is because she can't change her dad and his concept of who she should be. Acceptance of the fact that she can't change him will make the wall disappear.

Scotty dog says the pain is from walking through life feeling that whenever she made an average mistake she let her dad down. Dad thought she was a miracle and she should be perfect. Early in his marriage his wife had an abortion and he felt he would be punished for this. Scotty dog says don't talk to Dad about this yet until Sue works on it herself.

Leopard doesn't know how to react to this right now. She must walk through it with Bear and Scotty dog first. She must be stronger. She must be able to help Dad on his side of the wall first before she tackles this. As she becomes more comfortable with herself she'll become stronger. Things Dad expected of her she always expected of herself so she always failed because they weren't realistic.

At our next session Sue is tired but doesn't know why. Things are better with Mom. Sue looks softer than usual.

In the visualization she first meets Scotty dog and tells him she's tired. Scotty dog tells her she really hasn't taken care of herself this week. She's been playing rescuer. And now that she's more aware she'll begin to get tireder quicker.

"No matter how hard it is we can help people but we can't rescue them from themselves. My tiredness is a sign of my growth. Being in tune makes it impossible for me to get in a bad role for very long.

"I picked the Scotty dog up and we're going for a walk. We're in a forest. Bear and Leopard are there. Bear is very glad that I've come to rescue her. She's been sending me signals all week and she's tired. Leopard is not tired at all. It's just the Scotty dog and the bear. I ask Leopard why he isn't tired. He says because I haven't allowed him to do his work. He said I must become aware that people will hurt and that will hurt me but I can't fix other people's problems. I can only fix myself. Anyone close to me knows that if they hurt I'll step in and try to make things better. I must break that pattern. I can't take on someone else's pain.

"Some of the other tiredness I feel is just normal because I have no security in my life right now. I realize I'm leaving my job and going to a new one. I don't know if I'll go to Tacoma or Seattle. My thoughts and my plans are accurate but there's still a lot of stress I'm dealing with that's normal, and I've been reacting to that as well.

"Could the animals help you replenish your energy?" I ask.

"Bear says lay back on her and put everything else away. I've done about everything I can do. As far as being the rescuer I need to tell the person that I can't solve it for them. I must take the responsibility of them off of me. I need to take more quiet time for myself, get away by myself, if it's only for a drive. I have not looked to my own needs this week.

"My leopard has put his foot on my leg as he always

does as if to tell me that everything will be okay.

"My bear said to me if I need to rescue somebody, rescue her. She feels very good now. Leaning against her I feel her energy coming into me. Scotty dog said one of the reasons this happened is that I'm so aware that I'm almost too aware of other people's feelings before I'm ready to handle it. I mirror other people's feelings and feel them inside me. He says I have to be cautious and not to try to look so deeply into other people right now. I must learn how to react to all mine first, swiftly. He laughs and tells me that I must not play the counselor until I can counsel myself.

"The sun is shining. It's warm out. I can see my seagull flying around, doing all kinds of flips and nose dives. Scotty dog is telling him he better cool it a bit. It's neat to be free but he must also use his head and be cautious.

"It's the first time I've seen Alligator in a long time. He said he's been on a long sleep and that it's time he'll be helping the leopard with some of my reactions, and to be aware that he may be in contact with me about some of my reactions. It's kind of like a mystery. He's not telling me what kind of reactions. He says I'll know. He says in the past he's had to give me a lot of pain because I haven't listened to my signals and let my reactions come. He said the bear will send me all kinds of signals, she always does, way in advance before I get into trouble, and if I allow the leopard to do his work in his swiftness I'll feel less and less pain with myself. That's all he has to tell me. He's walking off now.

"And I'm feeling rested and stronger. It's like the four of us are laying in the sun in contact with one another. Bear is strong again. Scotty dog wants to play with a toy. Leopard is ready for action.

"Bear said that I should be cautious and to try to be

with them before I make big decisions that might be scary. That I'm very vulnerable at this time in my growth. You can look at the people around you as a mirror of yourself only, not as a tool to change anyone except yourself. Bear needs to go see about her baby so she's going to leave now. She's letting her baby explore the world like I am mine, and that's part of growing up. You won't always be there.

"I pick up Scotty dog and walk back with Leopard. Leopard says it's time for him to go now, but that he'll be with me. When I don't know what to do to take a deep breath and let it happen. He'll do the work. I must allow it to happen.

"Scotty dog refreshes my memory that not too long ago it was me and him alone. He wants me always to remember where I came from because it's such a different place from where we are today. Before we were separate. He was working hard and I was working hard, but we weren't together. Now we're together.

At the beginning of our next session, Sue told me she was able to share openly, express emotion, and cry with a friend during last week. She had never done this before, feeling always that she had to be strong, that emotions were not to be openly displayed.

In her visualization, Crocodile wants to know what it felt like to let go of some emotions. He's excited to know that she was able to do this.

"It's one thing to know what your emotions are and where they're coming from, but letting go of them is something I've never done. He's going to help me with that. Not only to let the leopard swiftly make decisions on my emotions, but to let my emotions out. To not let our emotions out is as bad as not acting on them.

"He wants me to remember about the last time we

talked — that if you don't let your emotions out or let yourself feel what you feel, it is pain. It's another way of releasing and gaining energy.

"Scotty dog comes running up and seems happy that I'm learning to share my emotions. Being able to share sadness or confusion is also a sign of growth. I must never pretend what I don't feel. I pretend to be okay when I'm not okay. When I get signals and allow my body to react to those signals, another step is knowing when to let go of certain things.

"Scotty dog said, 'Think of your mother, how most of her whole world is a pretense of what's really not happening or what she's not feeling. Games of being okay when she really wants to scream that she's not okay.' I grew into that game, now I must grow out of it.

"He said, 'Think of what your mother said a few days ago.' I asked my mother why she doesn't communicate what she feels, why she doesn't stand up to my dad. Her answer was if she had done it a long time ago they probably wouldn't be together today.

"We're going to meet the other animals. Leopard and Bear are in their usual spot in the forest. The leopard wants to take me through the sequence of events. Leopard says that Bear gave me signals of uncomfortableness. My decisions were to get rid of that uncomfortableness and I let him take me swiftly to a place where I could release those emotions and the alligator released the emotions and Scotty dog let me know it was okay. It's okay to have wants and needs rather than trying to meet everyone else's wants and needs. Bear says I've always lived as if it were better to give than to receive so I never allowed myself to receive. If you don't release you can't receive. So I was always running out of fuel.

"Seagull comes to join us. He tells me it's nice to be able to think clearly. I've had a lot of confusion this week about certain things that I need to do and Seagull's telling me that I'm making it more confusing. Seagull tells me to do what my first impression is, that usually your first instinct is the truest. When I ponder and ponder he flies around in circles. Your first instinct, good or bad, saves a lot of time and energy and it's usually correct. Decisions are quick actions, not thinking and thinking. He's flying off, saying, 'No pondering this week. Go by your first impressions.'

"I'm leaning against my bear. She's very calm. She's saying to me that for so many years I've been like her baby cub. She's been trying to get him to do things over and over. She tries to get him to stay close to her and he runs off. When I stay close to her the signals are clear.

"Scotty dog says no emotions are bad. Even no thoughts are bad. It is the actions that sometimes have to be altered. That who I am is everything in me. Scotty dog says, 'Do you want a life or just smiles? Do you want to just be able to handle yourself smiling?'

"No, I don't. I want to be able to handle the whole me. Scotty dog doesn't want me to be hard on myself.

"Scotty dog says I had no guidance in how to handle hurt feelings or sad feelings. You can't find your way across the U.S. if you don't have a road map. Or if you can't read your car gauge you'll find yourself on empty. My emotions have been running on empty.

"I understand something that's happening. In my throat rather than a frog is a King Cobra. And it frightens me. I find myself pressing hard against my bear. My bear says not to be afraid. That they want my emotions to come out of my mouth as if it were cunning and quick and viperous, so I can learn speed in speaking my feelings. That the cobra is not dangerous unless it bites. That there's come a time that I must get rid of the danger inside me and quit poisoning myself. With the slightest tap, the slightest crackle, cobra's ready to strike. I must turn that way not in the context of striking at people or cutting with words, but only in the context of speed and getting rid of the poison, accuracy. I may find things coming out of my mouth that I don't want to come out but they will come out.

"Bear says she uses snakes sometimes for her cub, to teach him what he should stay away from and that danger can be very quick.

"I really hate snakes. Bear says that's exactly why the cobra is my emotions. Because I hate to let anybody know I had them.

"The snake is gone now.

"The bear says not to fear the snake. That if it gets out of hand they'll be there. They feel they must do something drastic for me to become aware of the many times I've wanted to grow and that I would not let myself grow in my emotions, in letting people know I had them. That I must stay close to them because this is a real danger point.

"I'm telling my bear that I can't get over the feeling that some sort of reptile is in me, that I'll dream about it. She says, 'Don't worry. We want you to think about it.' That not showing my emotions is really going to kill me if I don't learn to do it. That as long as I share my emotions and don't let them build up this reptile will not emerge, because I'll be using him inside to attack these things and get rid of them. But if I don't, I'll feel a great fear inside, uncomfortableness, sickness.

"We're all working as one now.

"Leopard says that he wants me to touch his head and

lie back on the bear and he'll fill me full of energy, and when I
have a white, glowing light around my whole body I can let go
of him. The light is for protection. It's an energy shield. And in
my right hand he's placed a sword. And the sword is to protect
me against my emotions and the reptile. Now I feel safe. I feel
this glowing circle.

"The leopard said I'm ready to face the day. He wants
me to say goodbye to them.

At our next session Sue looked more solid than ever
before and she had a new haircut.

She says she has carried the golden glow all week. She
has been interacting with people who have pain but without
feeling she has to do something. She hasn't been assuming
responsibility for their pain.

As her visualization begins she says, "The animals are
all here, having a party. They're all happy and energetic, all
gathered to greet me. Leopard is the first one to greet me. He
wants to know how it feels to have enough power to do
anything I choose to do. I think it's great. So does he. It's like
all of my animals are energized.

"And here's the seagull. It's been so great that he's been
able to think. I haven't been pondering over anything. I've been
reacting.

"They all want to talk at once. They all want to get my
attention at once.

"Scotty dog says, 'You're not feeling tired today, are
you?'

"No. I haven't been getting snagged in things. I haven't
been worrying about decisions. Just letting them flow.

"Leopard is curious to know my relationship with
Cobra. I'm still very frightened of Cobra. I don't want him to

appear. But when he appears, I'm aware I need to do something and I do it. Leopard is smiling.

"'Now you know why I used the Cobra. Now do you know how much better it can be if you don't hold onto these things?'

"How long will Cobra be there?" I asked.

"Leopard says, 'For as long as it needs to be. For as long as you need a reminder that you need to act.'

"Alligator is nipping at my ankles. He says he really feels good that he hasn't had to bite at me. I'm letting him do his work. He really doesn't want me to feel any pain. He gets along great when he gets to do what he needs to do.

"Giraffe is admiring herself in a big crystal clear pond. Now I know what she does. She's proud of herself, she likes herself. She's not running from herself anymore. She used to always be nervous that something was going to jump on her or kill her. She's very different now. Like she's come out of a big, dark place. She's like a little kid.

"My bear wants me to come over and see her. I give her a great big hug. She's such a neat animal. She's saying that I've been making her job less taxing all the time. She's had much more time to sun herself and hunt for berries. She hasn't had to save me from some dilemma every two minutes. She's not sarcastic anymore.

"She's saying she wants me to become conscious and be more patient with my mother, and let her be who she is, that she's okay. And try to never be short with her. And to be conscious of the colors around her. To really look around her and be conscious of the colors around her. That someone will tell me what those colors mean.

"I've told her I've become so aware of every flaw in my dad and I don't like that. She says soon I'll begin to work on what I like when I know what I don't like. As I become more conscious of soft people's colors, like my mom, I will grow more aware of seeing colors of people that are hard. That will come later. I must keep a diary this week of all I see and I must not be afraid to reach out and touch those colors. And soon I'll become aware of what the soft whitish glow around me resembles.

"Leopard is nudging his face under my arm. He's saying to sit down with my legs in an Indian position and again put my left hand on his head. And again feel his energy even stronger flowing through my circle of energy and that in my right hand I still have my sword. This is a golden sword. It's a special sword with a double edged blade: one side is for strength and the other side is for empathy and goodness. Strength to do what I need to do, and I can also use it to do battle, and I must know which side to use. That all through my life I've only had a single sided sword.

"I feel close to all my animals, but very special about this leopard. Leopard says I've been very close to them and I'm getting closer all the time. I still fall asleep but I'm at least able to make a short contact with Scotty dog. He tells me someday I'll be able to contact any of them when I need to."

Chapter Twelve
The Bridge and the Sword

At this time in my work I purchased a tape recorder and began taping the imagery sessions. The following three sessions, which are also the last three I did with Sue, were transcribed directly from cassette tapes recorded at the sessions. The previous chapters were taken from written notes, and because of the easy cadence of Sue's speech during imagery I was able to maintain a good record of our work together. The difference that comes through clearly is the nature of her opening expression, before the visualization begins, which is much more full and thorough on the tapes.

"My animals told me I should watch for colors around people, and I haven't seen any. I've come to the conclusion I'm not supposed to force it. Maybe getting to know my mom better through imagery I'll begin to see them. I can feel her softening now. I'm feeling more with my feelings.

"I've been in touch with my animals more than ever. When I want them I can just be with them. I don't even have to go through the relaxation. It's just really been weird, because always before I had to lay down and then I'd almost be able to contact Scotty dog, and then it would cut off, I'd fall asleep. But now when I want one of them there it's like I can put my hand on one of them. I'm really sensitive right now.

"This is how my whole week's gone, it's just been one thing after another. Monday I went to the Post Office and there was a letter from X___ College and I thought to myself there's only 17 people that are accepted out of two hundred aplicants in the X___ College counseling program so I never really felt that I had much chance getting in. So I opened the letter and I thought to myself, 'Well, this is my rejection letter.' And the first line was 'You've been accepted into the counseling program.' And I must have read that five times. It couldn't sink into my brain that you've been accepted if you want to go. So Tuesday I went over and talked to them and it's like my direction is to go there. My course load would be 10 or 11 units per quarter. And then I thought, 'Do I want to go there?' And, 'Yes, I want to go there.'

"And then I thought, 'Well, I have to have a job.' So it's been like I've been putting all these little blocks in my way and God is removing them faster than I can put them. I went to the office and the personnel director gave me names of people she knew who could give me a job.

"My sword and my energy cell: I'm becoming more and more aware of them all the time. When I get in trouble I become warm all over my body and then I say what I feel. Sometimes I think, 'What did I say that for?' But it's almost spontaneous. If I feel a feeling and it's something that I need to express, I express it, whether it be to a friend or whatever.

"I spent a week writing an essay on alcoholism and presented it to a professor and he started marking on it, 'Now, you need to do this, you need to do that, we don't need to hear about these steps, change them so that they're more geared to a person you're talking to in your essay rather than to a group, change the wording of it.'

"I said, 'I can't do that, Sir.'

"And he said, 'Well, why can't you? And in spite of what you say, you've written here that there's no completely successful program without entering AA. There's never a 'no'!'

"And I said, 'What? Can you tell me what qualifies you for making that decision?'

"He said, 'Well, I don't have to qualify.'

"I said, 'Well, I'll tell you something. I'm qualified to make that because I'm a recovering alcoholic of eight years, and I have been on the program eight years. I've seen a lot of people come and go and we've buried a lot of people that thought they didn't need the program.'

"And he apologized all over the place. He just backed up like I'd backed him right into a wall. He must have talked to me for half an hour about how sorry he was and then he went into the situation about his wife and that her family is all alcoholics, and how she gets upset if he just has one or two beers, anything out of the ordinary frightens her. And he asked me some things about what he could do and how he could deal with it. An unbelievable situation. Then he handed me my paper after he'd marked all over it, here it was neatly typed, and he said, 'I'm really sorry. I need to be more careful in tearing into people's things without aknowledging that they know where they're coming from.'

"And I said, 'Yeah, maybe you do. Because I wrote this from my heart and my experience, because I've been there and I am there. It was very threatening to me that you attacked my program and it's the reason that I'm here and able to write it.'

"And he hands me my paper like a little kid and says, 'I'm really sorry that I marked on it.'

"And I said, 'Well, Dr. ____, if you expect me to retype this by tonight, forget it, I'm not going to.'

"He said, 'You have until Monday to get it in.'

"This is my energy cell and my sword. This is what happens to me now. If I get into a situation, I face it immediately. And if that's uncomfortable, I'm going to deal with it. It's almost like I have no control over dealing with it or not dealing with it. Always before people have attacked my program, or I've sat around and let people talk about alcoholics and I've wanted to jump up and say 'You don't know what you're talking about!' but I never have. It's always been like, 'Well, if you say you're an alcoholic, you're threatening your position.' And I feel like today, 'No, that's an asset of who I am today.' And if they don't understand, if they choose not to understand it, that's their problem. And if it jeopardizes some situation that I'm in, maybe I'd better not be in that situation.

"It's kind of like my whole aspect on who I am and who I feel I am, and how I identify with who I am is different. I'm beginning to know who I really am today. And I like it. And I don't want to hide it. It's like I can't hide it. That came out of my mouth so quick I couldn't stop it or even think, 'Oh, I shouldn't have said that. That's a situation where you could end up getting an F for that class for doing that.' I really let him have it. And it worked out well. I guess it was supposed to happen. But that's just an example of the what's been happening to me.

"The one thing on my mind today, and I don't know why it's there, I want to deal with, or try to deal with, with my animals, any negative vibrations I might have that might be standing in my way of dealing with these decisions. Still part of me is trying to say, 'This is safe. Make this decision. Stay here.' And a bigger part of me is saying, 'Hey. It's okay. That's the direction in which you're supposed to go. You're 39 years old, get on with it.' And a little voice inside keeps saying, 'You won't be able to find a job, you're going to be all frightened, it's going to be all new people.' And I'm having a difficult time getting rid of that little fear. I realize all of us have that but I think what I'm saying is I want to deal with it before it grows. I feel like it might have a tendency to grow. It's okay to be a little fearful, but I don't want it to become uncontrollable.

"And I don't know if it's too much to deal with, but I also want to quit smoking. I can put 'em aside for two or three days and then the first thing you know I'm smoking another cigarette, and I hate it and I want to stop it."

At this point we proceeded with the brief relaxation with which I begin each visualization session.

"Take a deep breath and allow your eyes to close. Give your body permission to relax and be comfortable. Allow your body to experience the contact that it makes with the chair and with the floor, and let it adjust itself in any way it needs to in order to be fully comfortable.

"And as you tune in to the rhythm of your breathing imagine that when you inhale you're inhaling a little bit of the sky, and it's very clear and very refreshing. As you inhale let the sky fill your body with those qualities, fill your being with those qualitites. And as you exhale imagine that you're letting go of everything that's old and stale and stressful, everything that's ready to be let go of, letting go just easily and naturally. So that the rhythm of your breathing is seen as that beautiful process of taking in what's fresh and clear, and letting go of what's no longer needed.

"Allow your imagination to be open and receptive, and let yourself go to meet with your animals wherever they may be, and tell me when you first see them."

"I'm with them. Actually, I was with my Scotty dog the whole time you were taking me through the relaxation. He was jumping up and down, couldn't wait for me to be there. Every time I meet with him it's a feeling like being away from home for a period of time and how you get very anxious and excited about going home. Gee, it's like there's an excitement in the air, in the breeze, in the leaves of the trees. It's like our forest is all lit up with energy and strength. My Scotty dog is so excited today. I'll ask him what he's so excited about.

"He's excited about all my doors opening. He just won't stay still today. It's like I've been gone a long time and he's so excited and jumping around. I caught him in mid-air during one of his jumps. The whole forest is excited about my growth and energy. About my willingness to give to myself as well as others. Every area of my life has grown. He wonders if I know that. And I do.

"He's very excited about the fact that I'm working with Mom. This is what he's really excited about.

"He said that we have always needed to be able to give. But because we didn't know in what area or what direction to give, we have always given of ourselves, rather than our strength, because we had no strength to share. And that I can learn to share my strength and not give up part of myself. That my strength is all I really can give people, and my experience and hope. But as far as something tangible that they can hold onto, it's my strength. But my hopes are not yet their hopes until they have strength. And my experience is only a bridge to tie to their bridge. Our common experience is to know how to walk in one another's paths.

"Scotty dog says I've always had a beautiful gift of insight into people. He says I've allowed myself to walk inside a person's house I barely knew, and to walk inside the house of a person I love very much. And the pain is quite the same. And the reason it's the same is I'm allowing them only to draw from my strength. And that's the task that I needed to know, feel, find out. If I step inside someone's house, by that they mean their body, their emotions, and allow them to hook me in their pain, and I lose my strength — then that's what used to always happen to me. I had very little to begin with but when I got hooked, then I didn't have any.

"He's telling me I'm generating strength from

everyone, and I'm beginning to have the relationships where you continue to draw strength. There is a great deal of strength in pain.

"I ask my Scotty dog what I need to do with these people.

"He said, 'Be a guide', like he's been my own guide, 'until they have their own guides.' And I will find myself growing more and more: the more I give the more I grow. That it's like a little heater inside me.

"It's kind of funny, the Leopard's almost putting his big paw in the Scotty dog's mouth. It's like, 'It's my turn. I want to talk to her, too.'

"My hands are very warm right now, like I'm being energized. The leopard has an energy radiance around him. He's asking me how it feels to be warm with him. Really, warm with all my animals. I think it's neat. I love to feel my leopard, it's so velvety, so sleek, so proud. I'd like to give him a big hug.

"It's unbelievable, hugging him my hands even get warmer. They really feel like they're radiating heat right now. Probably they are. He wants me to become more and more aware of how powerful he is. How much strength and control he has.

"He's asking me if I've seen the snake. And I say I haven't even thought about the King Cobra this week. I haven't seen him and I know why. He's smiling at me. He says I don't even have to ask him and I know why. It's because I'm reacting to my emotions. Almost like they come out before I think about them. I just ask him if it could happen, that I *do* say things I shouldn't say. He said no, I'm in control. He said there really isn't any emotion not worth expressing at the moment you feel it. It's your reaction sometimes that needs to be changed to that.

"He took me back to an instant this week when I did feel pain in expressing emotion. He asked me if I've changed my reactions to that pain. Yes I have. Needing to deal with that person in a different light. And I have. And it feels more comfortable now.

"It's like I'm seeing peeks at last week. I went right from there to sitting in Dr. ____'s office. The words that are coming from my mind: 'I do not regret the past and I do not wish to shut the door on it.' What this means to me is that I accept who I am. And I don't want to shut the door on who I am, whether it's my alcoholism, or that I cry easily, or whatever. The past is who I am, or part of who I am today.

"He said I got that a little wrong. It's, 'I do not wish to relive the past, nor do I want to shut the door on it.' I heard those words somewhere, read them somewhere. One of the AA promises. After step 9.

"He's telling me I should read those every day because every one of them has come true for me. My fear of economic insecurity has left me. It doesn't mean I have a million dollars in the bank, it just means I know I can make it no matter what.

"He just put his paw on my leg 'cause he knows that was a very sensitive thing I just said. I didn't think I would ever say that, but I know, no matter what, I'll make it. It's very neat to feel that and know that. That fear being gone. I want to talk to him about these little fears.

"My animals are beginning to — they can't seem to everybody get in what they want. The minute I said that my seagull came flying in, perched himself right on my leopard, my leopard took his paw and nudged him off, like they're battling for first place today, it's unbelievable.

"The thing he's chiding me about is quit going back

and forth. I know which program is the easiest for me, the best for me. It's really better that I go to X___ College. What am I trying to do, stay here and kill myself, trying to take all these hours? He's really irritated at me. It's almost like he's taking one of his feet, like you do to a kid when you take your finger and you shake it at him. He's saying quit dilly-dallying around and get your confidence together and do it. He's saying we'll all be there together. I won't be alone.

"When I used to make these moves before I *was* alone because I was alone inside my own house. I had no friends in there, therefore I had no confidence, no faith in myself, just a bunch of fear. He's saying that I don't have that now, what I have is an apprehension about making the right decision. At 39 years old, you can't afford to mess up. That's what I'm dealing with.

"He's saying, 'Yes, that is a fear.' In jobs I have to look at it logically, some things are logical. If I have to, put both things on two separate pieces of paper. Look at the hours, the benefits, the drawbacks. And the one that's got the most, wins. It's that simple. And then once you make the decision, then the next decision is to go over and get a job. And then when you have a job you move over. It's a sequence thing, it's not all mashed together.

"He's like this little old professor telling me now this is the way to do it. It's so funny, he's usually not like that. He's saying now he has too many things to do to keep talking to me. This is what I need to do, just do it. He's getting tired of being interrupted all the time by all these back and forth things, mind trips.

"He says I'm doing better but now he gets real irritated real easy. He says he really doesn't mean to but it's just that he was locked up for such a long time and when you get a little freedom, you want it all the time. It's not that I'm not on schedule it's just that he wants to always be riding on these big wings because he likes to have lots of time to play.

"My bear is immediately going to something different. She's saying that I must be very gentle with my mom. For even though she knows that the best place for me is over in California, she's having a difficult time letting go of me. And that I can help her smooth that out inside herself. I've always been there for her, and maybe I can help her learn how to be there for herself. It's a special time that my mom and I will share, and that she will grow because she wants to grow. But to be especially careful at this time of her letting go of me. She said that she's felt that for me, letting go, when I let go of Bobby. And I'm still letting go of Bobby. So I know what that is to feel. So I can be more sensitive how that feels now. To just be careful, and slow, and gentle with her. She needs a lot of strokes.

"My alligator just growled to get my attention. This is really funny: he's smoking a cigar. He said, 'I look pretty ridiculous, huh?'

"Yeah, he really looks ridiculous.

"He said that's about how ridiculous it is for *me* to smoke. This is really weird since I haven't talked at all about it. At least not to the alligator. Sometimes I call him an alligator and sometimes I call him a crocodile. I ask him what he is really.

"He says, 'Alligator, crocodile, alligator, what's the difference?' He's really funny today.

"I ask him to get serious about my smoking.

"He said it's an emotional release to anxiety. That I'm smoking *at* my problems. Not smoking because I like it or enjoy it or any of those things. I'm smoking at it. Like you become angry at something so you do something hateful towards it.

"He says the reason that I'm disliking it more all the time is that I'm building my strength against cigarettes. And that soon, very soon, I can just throw them away. But that won't be today, it will be soon. When I'm ready it'll just happen. I just won't pick them up. He said he could take that habit away if he wanted to right now, but so many of my little blankets have been taken away that he chooses not to do that today. That's one of my little security blankets, that I'll do my smoking. That every day I'm getting closer. But that he wanted me to really feel how ridiculous it is. And that in itself is enough for today. That it is coming, and it will be soon.

"He spit the cigar out. He said he wanted to get serious for a minute. I've never thought of him as being funny but he's sure funny today.

"He's also taking me back to some situation. He said, 'Nice going, you did a good job. Nobody cut our emotions off, nobody said that's not okay, we did what we felt, expressed what we felt, and it's okay.' Aha. He said to me, 'This is something you must always be aware that other people have the right to do, too. That two people can have opposite feelings on the very same subject, and theirs is okay and yours is okay. That's the ability to allow the other person to feel theirs, too, and then to allow you to feel yours.' And as I get more in tune to these feelings I'll become more in tune to other people needing to feel theirs. And that I'll work on that a little this week. He said I have too much of an urgency sometimes for people to know how I feel and I don't listen to how they feel. I need to try that a little.

"My giraffe is just running up the lane. She has flowers stuck in her horns, her little horns by her ears. And she's been out admiring herself. She says she's really sorry she's late, but being late for being good to yourself once in awhile is okay. 'Break some old habit,' she says. 'Do something a little different, be a little different. People won't understand because they're so used to you doing things in certain ways at certain times.'

"She's really changed so much. She used to be so frightened and scared. Like she was running all the time. Muscles on her back were tense, and you could feel them move. She's not that way anymore. Kind of happy go lucky, jolly. She says she's really happy for us.

"I noticed all my animals are using us. It's not them and I anymore, it's *us*. We do this and we do that. Us together. I don't look at them so much as a part of me, I look at them as me. They *are* me.

"And as I look at them I'm up above them looking down. They're kind of a neat bunch, a lot of warmth and strength.

"That was a wierd experience! All of a sudden I landed on the ground! The leopard's saying he's really sorry, he just lost his concentration for a minute. He must have put me up there. He just wants me to be alert. 'Don't always trust what you see, but you can always trust what you feel. Learn how to land on your feet. Learn that I may not always be right there that second, you have to rely on something else.'

"It's time for me to draw from his strength again. He's having me put my left hand on his head, and he's right next to me. His head is on my lap and we draw from his strength. We're all gathered around in a little circle, all our faces together, very much into what we're doing. It's like through me they're all being energized. I feel his energy passing through me.

"He's giving me my gold sword again and he's telling

me to tap each one of my animals on the head and give them some energy also. And as they're coming forward I move the sword and I feel my energy flow, they disappear. They disappear into my sword.

Now it's just me and the leopard. He's saying I have all the tools to successfully do anything I want to do. And that I'll begin to see energies as well as feel them. And that I must be conscious of what I'm seeing. Begin to trust and rely on myself. And he'll be just as far away as my energy. And that I'm ready to face the week. And he jumps into my sword.

Sue opened her eyes.

"That was really powerful. I could just feel their power from everywhere. I just feel tingly all over. Very alert. Very energized. Almost like I can get up and walk out of here and walk different. I feel different. I don't really know what it is. The thing that comes to my mind immediately is that I'm more one today than I ever have been. It's a feeling like a piece of me is not here and here and here. And that's how I've seen my animals, as pieces of me, one sitting here and one sitting here and one sitting here. All of a sudden it's *me, they are me.* That's really powerful. But that's what it feels like. It doesn't feel like I'm leaving them today, It feels like I'm carrying them."

"I saw something change in you as they entered your sword: your eyes, the color of your face," I said.

"I wish that it could be put into words. It was almost like I could see, feel, my heart entering me, and my strength entering me, my mind entering me. It's almost like looking down on yourself and seeing yourself come together, feel yourself come together. And I can feel the hairs on my arms standing up and I'm not cold, it's just... I think it's so overwhelming I don't think it's really... really hasn't attached me yet, what I really feel, as far as being able to put it into words. I can feel it there but it's so big and so powerful I can't put the right words to how I feel. It's like just sitting there in wonderment.

"The closest thing I've ever felt like that in my life is when my grandfather passed away. He was so close to me. I loved him so much. I went out to his grave that night. It was cold. It was winter. And the flowers on his grave were warm, and he'd been buried for hours. And all of a sudden a light came down from the heavens and it was just on his grave. And in an instant it was gone. I spent a lot of time trying to find out what that was. Until I finally realized it was his spirit. I actually saw my grandfather's spirit. And that overwhelming feeling of I don't know what it is. It was so powerful that it can't be expressed in single short words or phrases. Now I feel different sitting here. It's really exciting. I could move mountains today. It's a real strength.

"As I was looking down on my animals today, before my leopard let me drop on the ground, it was like, 'That's my personality, and I like it, that's my heart and I really like it', or my energy, my strength, my power is so sleek and soft and gigantic in a neat way. It was like all of a sudden in a split second I was given the opportunity to see individually what I am, and just as fast to be plunked down. Kind of as a realization I feel like the leopard was saying, 'Respect it, respect who you are, learn to stand on your own two feet, on who you are, because they can destroy you too if you don't respect them.' That's what I've been feeling.

"I become more and more aware all the time of what they mean when they say something to me. It's almost like we get into a conversation and I know what the outcome is before it's said. Almost like fine tuning. Like a little bulb goes on in my brain, aha, this is where it's supposed to go before it's said. What they talked about, moving to California, that fear of not making the right decision, you could not make any decision. What I got from that, what I'm feeling about that is, whatever decision it is, it's right. Both of them are right. It's whichever of them is easier to obtain. The seagull made that so plain. They're both right. Quit going back and forth about it, put them down on a piece of paper and see which of them is "gooder" for you, which one fits. If you can't do that in your mind, put it on paper. And that's where it is. It's that simple, but it's true.

"And the alligator saying that I need to become aware, fine tune myself, it's okay for me to feel and it's okay for someone else to feel too. Don't stop their growth. Don't stop them from feeling what they feel too. Just because you feel differently doesn't mean that they're wrong or you're wrong.

"And another thing that they said that really struck home for me: allow that person to feel what they feel, and by the same token, be around people who allow you to feel what you feel too. There are some people who won't allow it, because they're not in your space. You kind of have to know what it's like to be allowed those feelings and not be allowed those feelings to know when a person is cutting those off.

"I didn't realize that until I started coming here. I knew a lot of people that cut my feelings off. Those people I must stay away from. At least not be around them except on a limited basis. Because they stifle my growth. I can be aware of who those people are now. Maybe someday they'll grow into a space that then we can communicate. But until then there's really no need. It's kind of an empty valley for both of us. If you can't meet in a happy medium and share where each other is then there's really no need in sharing, trying to share. I feel that very strongly today. And that I'll know where I'm supposed to be with those people.

"I feel like I've got a whole bunch of new knowledge that I'm going to be trying out.

"A thought that just came to me right now is that from now on when I visit my animals they'll be coming *out* of me to visit. It's a different feeling. Like I've allowed them to come home. That's powerful. That feels like a lot of power in me.

"It feels like I've grown to about ten feet today. Like a party going on inside. Like a big release, a big release. I walked in here today knowing myself better. I feel like I'm walking out of here with my whole self. I don't feel like I'm leaving part of me here. That's exciting. It's really neat.

At this point our session ended. The total session lasted an hour and fifteen minutes.

Chapter Thirteen
The Mountain

" **M**y animals truly are one, now. It's really exciting. I don't even know whether they'll even come out because they're in there, there's nothing for them to come out to. Does that make sense? I mean, I can talk to them any time I want to, now.

"Like last night. I'm going to drive to San Francisco today after I leave, and I had a big test today, and I was able to communicate - rather than me stepping out and visiting my animals, I stepped in - I don't know whether you know what I'm talking about - and I was just able to hug them and talk to them, just like I was talking to myself, they were just there, there was no effort to it. It's like I laid down and closed my eyes and I started talking to them and Scotty dog was right there. And it was just like I went through them, my emotions, my power animal, the whole gamut of my animals, and I had something to say to them of what I needed from them and what they were doing for me. And we talked about the fact that we are one, that I don't have to search for them, I don't have to look for them. I carry them with me all the time, now. I don't have to have a special place to get down and concentrate on meeting with them because they're with me all the time, as one. It's really a neat feeling. It's hard to explain how that feels. Instantaneously now, my emotions will click right in, and my actions to what I need to do about them. If I have a feeling I know why I have that feeling. It's not masqueraded by — If I'm hurt, it's not masqueraded by anything, I know it's hurt, and I know why it's hurt, and I know why it's there. I'm not explaining this well, but it's really a different experience. It's like all of a sudden I have powers that

I didn't know I had before.

"Yesterday my mom was laying on the sofa, she was laying there asleep, and I began to scan her body, and the thing that came to me that I never understood before, and I know it's my animals telling me this instinctively, she has fears — I'm going to go get my son's new car and trade him cars, and I'm going to bring it back here and I'm going to sell it and trade it for a little better car than I've had. Then when I go to X___ College I'll have a little better transportation, more dependable. And she doesn't want me to sell that new car because she knows that as long as I have that that I'm going to be safe, and I'm going to be able to come home when she needs me. And I've had a difficult time explaining to her that if I'm in a different car I'll be okay. While I scanned her it was like I was able to step inside her and find out that she's not in the same space I'm in. She's 65 years old. She doesn't think like I do. And for the first time I was able to see my mother as 65! I've been seeing her as 40. I've been expecting her to react to my questions and what-not as a 40 year old. She's not 40 years old any more. She's sixty-five. She doesn't think like she did 20 years ago. *I'm* the one that's almost 40. She's a very special lady getting old, she's getting old. And for a minute it was almost scary, I could almost see her in her casket. It was like 'accept your mother where she is, enjoy her where she is. You can't bring her back to when she was forty years old, you can't expect her to be there. Accept where she is. Help her accept where she is. She's a tired little old lady.' I had never seen that before. The years have almost slipped by me. I think that's why I almost saw her in a death situation. It was like, 'Sue, this is where your mom is. Don't make her something she's not. Accept where she's at.'

"So I skipped a class last night, and while she was

sleeping I cleaned the house for her and did the dishes. It was like I'd been looking at Mom and thinking, 'How come Mom doesn't clean house like she used to? How come Mom doesn't get the breakfast dishes done until dinner? How come Mom sleeps all the time?' All of a sudden my animals, my spirit, was able to show me, 'She's older! She's tireder! And you better see that!' The rest of my day was very emotional for me.

"It's part of where I've been with my dad also. Part of the strain between my dad and I has been the inability to see that he's older. He's not a young man anymore. And I've wanted to take him back to when he was thirty and say to him 'why can't you react this way to me.' What I haven't taken into consideration is my dad's nearly sixty. He's an older man now. He's completely different than he was when he was thirty or forty, and I'm looking at him like when he was thirty, when he wasn't there. Maybe he is there now! And I haven't searched that out.

"It's like I've grown, and all the time I've grown my parents haven't grown in my mind. And all of a sudden I was able to say, 'Don't worry, you're the one that's almost forty. They're much older, and you'd better see that, because you're seeing through eyes twenty years ago.'

"And the feeling is very powerful. 'Get with it! You're grown. They have, too. They didn't stay there. You may have.' I think what I'm saying is for twenty years I've stayed at the same place, they haven't. And all of a sudden I've caught up with where they're at. And something's totally different.

"Night before last I went and got some hot fudge sundaes and brought them home after class, brought them home to Mom and Dad, and it's like my dad was a little kid, 'How did you know what I wanted? That's just what I wanted!' It was like another layer of that screen got pulled off."

119

"And how did you happen to bring him the sundae?" I asked.

"Because I knew that would make him happy. It would be a neat thing to do. But I hadn't wanted to do those things, and now I want to do them. And it's a neat feeling.

"There's an insight, and a growth, and a power in the imagery that's very beautiful. I was laying in bed last night as I was talking to my animals, and I choose to think of it as talking to my soul, parts of my soul, and I asked my leopard, 'Fill me again, full of your energy.' And I was able to lay there and watch and feel the energy. I put my hands around him and felt my hands begin to get warm, and the warmth goes up my arms and through my body, and ended up through my feet, and I'm a cold person when I go to bed. I know that I'm filling myself with that energy because I begin to get warm. And I can't lay there without doing that and get warm since I don't have the very best circulation. And so it's proving something happened inside me. And sometimes I need a proven situation like that to say to myself, 'Now, under normal circumstances you could not do this.'" Laughing, Sue said, "I have to do that to myself so I know it's real."

"And I'm glad you didn't give me those articles earlier (on the chakra animal work) because after reading some of those I saw that my imagery had become "like" some of them. I sat down and I thought to myself after I read that one article and parts of the book, 'Well, which animal is really your power animal? Which animal is really your earth animal?" I know my leopard must be my power, my power, the energy."

I said, "Well, I've done something with you that I hadn't done, that's not in the article. We started out with your hands, remember?"

"Uh huh."

"I had explored that with a couple of other people and then I started out that way with you, and that's what led us to what was going on. Remember that German Shepherd? And your Scotty dog?"

She replied, "And I found out that the Scotty dog was my heart. And that Shepherd, that deformed Shepherd I'd like to call him because he had the head of a wild animal, ended up turning into the leopard."

"Right", I said.

"So that had to have been my power."

I continued, "You know something a bit more complex. The work I did in the article began with some theoretical stuff and that's fine, but we are who we are. We aren't built according to some theory. Theory might be derived after we scan ourselves, and acknowledge some things about ourselves, but we are more fundamental than a theory. Theory comes from us, it's not that we're structured according to some theory. So what we're working with here is something more subtle and more complex than that particular theory. It's related to it."

"But it's not me", she said.

"It's not you."

"So I really shouldn't worry about it."

I replied, "No. You're right exactly where you are. And besides, they all work together, all the animals. If you go up to them and another one is needed, *they* put you in touch with it, or the other one comes forth. It's not necessary to know intellectually. Besides, that's really a narrowing of them. They're much more than anything we could describe. They're much more than any single function like that, much more: richer, deeper, fuller."

Sue said, "Then it's just kind of like, they're not separate. They've always worked as one. And it's really a unique neat thing. Because I haven't had to ponder around trying to find the one animal that was going to help me, because if the one I'm with can't, it's going to find the one that can."

"And the stuff I talked about in the article, the integration and so on, in you it just takes place spontaneously", I said.

Sue continued, "It's that they are so loving. There's always a lot of hugging and closeness, feeling and contact.

"My giraffe is growing more than any of them. And I feel that she is the part of me that didn't like me. I didn't like myself. Didn't like the way I looked, or wished that I could be different somehow. She's kind of — well, she's really grown, she's like, 'I like to admire myself, I'm okay,' she's not looking around for somebody to be poking at her, or frightened somebody's going to get her all the time. It's kind of like, 'Yeah, I'm okay.'

"I'm feeling that in me. As she's growing more and more, I'm feeling more and more okay. It's okay to experience how you feel, it's okay to be yourself. You don't have to be what everybody wants you to be. Be a little different. I feel her growing, and I feel myself growing.

"Fears that I have now about me I tend to think, 'Is that really you fearing that? No! It's my giraffe's fear.'

"One concept that I got from last week, that I've held onto and felt as I scanned my mom, and as I looked at my dad, and as I've had conversations with friends: to act aright, to express how you feel, isn't all; you must also have the acceptance: to accept what they feel. They may not feel what you feel, and that's okay. Most people spend all their lives, with their mate, their friends and whatever, trying to convince them their point of view. And your point of view comes from where you've been, how you've been raised, where you're going, who you are. And those places for that other person are different. There are going to be very few times that the other person is going to feel and think what you feel and think. It's okay for me today to be at the place that I'm at, and it's okay for you to be where you're at, too. So it boils down to communication, whether it's your mom, your lover, or whatever, of being able to communicate 'I feel this', and it also gave me the permission to feel what I feel. And it doesn't necessarily have to be the same. It's just being able to have the communication.

"Before I realized that, and believed that, and felt it, if I was with a person that I had a particular feeling about inside me, and you begin to know people pretty well, I would say to myself, 'Better not discuss that with them, because I already know how they're going to feel.' So the feeling would just be stuck inside of me. There's a real freedom of being able to go to that person and say, 'I know you're not going to be able to understand and feel where I'm at but I can communicate with you where I'm at. And I *know* you're going to be on a different level, you're going to be in a different place, and that's okay, too. But at least I can communicate with you where I'm at.' And it takes away the burden of stuffing that one more problem of feeling, of thought, until finally I could be stuck in it and never realize what you think or what you feel. And I've been saying that: 'I'd like you to give me the permission to tell you how I feel or where I'm at. And I understand you may not be there, and that's okay.' And there's a real freedom in saying that, I've found. And there's a real different kind of understanding when I look at you and I say, 'It's okay that you don't agree with me, because we're not in the same spot.' It's like they look at me and say, 'Gosh, I can have my own feelings about this.' You see a freedom in their face, too. As you are free, you give freedom to the other person. I *really* found that out. Because I've had some really deep, painful conversations with people, and through that they can come into a completely different place. It's like somebody opens a door that was shut a long time ago. It's really neat."

"I said to a friend, she started to talk to me about something and she said, 'I don't want you to get upset!' She said, 'I'm afraid you're going to get upset when I talk to you about this.'

"And I said to her, 'Give me the opportunity to show you that I'm not in that space anymore.' I said, 'I'll give you the freedom to feel however you want to feel if you'll give me the freedom to feel however I feel. And that doesn't mean that you're wrong and I'm right or vice versa, it just means that I'm going to give you the freedom to tell me how you feel, and it's okay no matter how you feel.'

"She looked at me like, 'You've gotta be kidding! I can really tell you how I feel?'

"We had about an hour and a half conversation about, 'It's okay. I understand.' And after she had expressed to me how she felt, I said, 'That's okay. This is where I'm at, and that's right for me, for now, and where you're at is right for you for now.' It was really a neat conversation, and out of that our friendship has grown. It's on a different plane from that one time of allowing each other to be honest and true with each other, and not feel like, 'I've got to convince her that I feel this way!' It took that burden away.

"And I've done that somewhat with my mom, too. I've taken the burden away from her, having to be something she's no longer, she's no longer that person anymore, she's different. And I think that I'm going to find a whole new life and

124

freedom with my dad. And I'm going to allow him to be where he's at and not keep putting him someplace where he's not. It's a real — I feel like I've been let out of jail. You can't expect a person to allow you any freedom you didn't ask for, and it's so easy to get into a groove of, 'I won't talk to that person because I know what they're feeling.' You have to go beyond that and say, 'It doesn't matter what they feel, that's okay for now. But I'll listen. And what I feel matters.' So I've been experiencing that all week.

"When I first came in I felt so tired. And I'm feeling more and more relaxed as I sit here."

"So You'll go to California?" I asked.

"Mmm hmm. I think to go in that direction is the best situation for me. It puts me closer toward where I want to be, faster."

"You start in September?"

"Mmm hmm. There's a very good possibility I may have a job already. It's director of a day school, pre-school."

"Wow!"

"Which I'm really excited about. This lady wanted to hire me over the phone. I think she could feel how I felt and my vibrations and I could feel hers. Our first meeting on the phone was very incredible. But maybe that's just something that's growing in me, too. I feel very good, it seems that's where I'm supposed to go. It's not going to be a very taxing job, it'll be a fun job, to work with little kids again. It'll be nice to do that. And I think there are some things I'll be able to do with imagery with these little kids, I'm going to try it out, and I'm excited about that. I think that's going to be a good move for me.

"It's kind of like I'm supposed to go back to working with kids for awhile. I think it'll be a real nurturing thing for me to do. So things that I didn't have the knowledge or the ability to do I'm going to do now. It's going to be a good experience for me.

"And if something else comes up, I can always do that, too. I want to work with some alcoholics over there. How and where, I don't know, but there's going to be a spot for that, too. It's like if you work with one person, then another one comes, and then another. It's like for some reason I'm supposed to do that, I'm supposed to get a lot of knowledge and strength in that area for something that I'm going to do later. What's supposed to happen will happen, naturally.

"That's funny. I've been the type of person that pushed and shoved everything together all my life, and now all of a sudden I'm not having to do any pushing or shoving. It's like if I'm supposed to be there, I'll be there, and I'll have all the tools and whatever I need to do it. And if I'm not supposed to I'm not going to push and shove it together anymore. That only puts me in a situation where I'm not supposed to be, and really uncomfortable. And I don't like to be uncomfortable anymore. If I feel the littlest bit of pain, I need to sit down and find out where it's coming from 'cause I don't like it. I'm so aware of when I'm in pain anymore. If my heart's in pain it's like my little Scotty dog grabs me and says, 'Hey, do something for me. I don't like this anymore.' Before when I was hurting, I didn't even know why. I didn't even have the slightest idea of what I needed to do to fix it. I feel like I don't have any screens around me anymore. Like my prison has been released."

"I think I would like to see what my animals are doing when I try to reach them today. So, I don't know whether I'm going to go see them, or....I just don't know what's going to happen. I know what happened last night, so...."

By this point in our therapy Sue had learned to relax

very readily, so my relaxation sugestions were quite brief.

"Just take a few deep breaths as you allow your eyes to close, and give yourself permission to relax and be fully comfortable sitting there. Allow your body to become aware of the contact that it makes with the floor and with the chair. And as you tune in to the rhythm of your breathing, imagine that every cell in your body is inhaling, directly, that pure sky, taking in that refreshing, cleansing energy, and letting go of anything that's old and stale, stressful, ready to be let go of. And allow yourself to go to meet with your animals, wherever they may be, and tell me when you can see them."

After a few moments Sue said, "I see a door. I'm supposed to go through the door.

"As I open the door it's like I'm looking at a gigantic me. It's a door to inside of me.

"It's to let me know that my spirit truly is all my animals. There's a place inside me where my spirit lies. And it's a beautiful place, very much like the spot where I always meet the animal's. And they're all there.

"The first animal that I'm closest to is the giraffe, and she puts her velvety nose on my shoulder. She says I've been more aware of her this week, because I've been working more on her this week. And feeling good about this. She said for the first time she feels full, like she's okay. Like she doesn't have to prove who she is. She doesn't have to be afraid that she's doing something wrong, or that she's in the wrong place, or that she's feeling something that needs to be changed. That whatever she is, she is, and it's okay.

"She says she's being closer with the other animals than ever before. It seems that wherever she walks, they walk.

"And Jonathan is right there. That's the seagull. He seems to be very alive, alert.

"I've got to sit by my leopard.

"He said before long I'll be becoming more and more aware of where my mom is. That she's almost a guide to where my dad is. My supersensitivity of who she is and where she is will make me realize and begin to feel that there's also that supersensitivity in my dad or she wouldn't be there. She gets angry at the fact that she hasn't been more aware of where she is and what she's felt and expressed that. But even hiding her feelings she wouldn't be with my dad if he was a really bad person, a really hard person, a really insensitive person. That what she meant the day she said that if she had expressed what she truly felt she and my dad wouldn't be together, what she really meant was it's too bad they didn't really get a deep feeling of where each other is, that they didn't really grow in all areas they could've together. But given the choice mom would've chosen dad again and again. That I must enjoy my times with my mom, and realize where she's at. There'll be those good and gentle times, helping times, closer times. That she's not going to always be there, and I have to enjoy the times that she is going to be there. That those times are precious. Now I begin to see colors around my mom. And her colors have been blocked out by my not understanding where she's at. Getting in tune with a person's energy level you must first get in tune with accepting them and their vibes and their space, and their relationship with you.

"I put my arm around my leopard. He tells me I'm beginning a journey, a journey of understanding where I am with Bobby. A journey to really look at him and see where's he's at. That he's not that little boy anymore. And to be able to transmit my strength and energies to him. That my energy has been building. That an overabundance will flow. From me other people will become energized and protected in their own feelings. That as my energy will be given to them I will even get great amounts of more energy.

"I see a mountain, a big mountain. Full of rocks and dark caves. And trees that are half-grown. And others that are immense. In places the mountain's very slick and treacherous. In other places there's snow. I've been walking this mountain for years. It's like I'm not on the mountain anymore, but I can see the mountain. I can see graves, and tears, lots of tears rolling down the mountain, and ghosts. And even a stream of blood flowing down the mountain, reddening the snow.

"Leopard's energizing my body. All the animals are gathered around. We're very close in a circle and we all have contact with one another. The leopard's put the gold sword in my hand and he's telling me to touch that mountain.

"And it's like I'm a gigantic person, I've grown larger than that mountain. And as I touch that mountain it's like a big volcanic explosion. I see big chunks of rock flying in the air, and the snow is melting. And I see a big energy ball over this demolished mountain. The leopard says that all our energy touched the snow. And as I touch the snow the mountain's disappearing, the fragments of it that are left. Then a river begins to flow, and trees begin to grow, and grass begins to grow on the earth, and the sun begins to shine, and I see small animals in the forest that's growing.

"I see my family, and each one of them as they come forth.

"My mom, and I tap her on the shoulder, and I give her the permission to be her.

"My dad's kneeling, and I give him the permission to be him. And my son permission to grow.

"And my granddaughter the strength to be strong.

"My son's wife the permission to be my son's strength

to help him grow, and she'll grow through this.

"And her son the permission that I accept who he is and that I accept him in my life.

"And Margaret, I give her my strength and I accept that there's nothing more I can do for her.

"And then Mary, and I give her permission to grow without me, and the strength, but I will be there as a friend.

"I see many other people I know and they're all saying to me, 'We accept you, and we allow you to be among the people you want to be with.'

"Leopard says I will be going down to the stream and I will cross it at a new depth. For these things I needed to let go of, each one was at a different level on my mountain bothering me; each one of these people had their separate hook in my growth. I'm free of this now.

"He said there are no more mountains for me to climb, only valleys. And if my valley for a short time turns into a mountain, I must contact my spirit and find out how to destroy that mountain, for there's no room for these things in my life anymore. Even through deep pain I'll be able to live in my valleys. It doesn't have to be a hard road to climb. Even in disaster it can be a journey, a journey into something new, to learn, to view.

"Again I feel the leopard's strength, his warmth, his courage to face anything, his positiveness. I feel the other animals, their strength, their guidance. He said again it's time for me to journey, and again I will feel them as I move on, and that they will be there. And if I want to contact any of them, anytime, at anyplace, they will be there.

"Leopard tells me to take my sword and to touch each of my animals. As I touch them they disappear into my sword, each of them. The giraffe is first. They come to the sword willingly, that's what they want to do, where they want to be. They want to be together. I have to lean down and touch my alligator and he disappears into my sword. As I reach out and touch my seagull it's like his energy breaks up into little swords. My bear gently walks into the sword. And my Scotty dog jumps into the sword.

"My leopard's standing before me and says that as soon as he disappears into the sword I'll be ready to face my travels, full of energy, full of anticipation of a new beginning. He says, 'Don't forget that I am here. I am as close as you just beckoning, to talk to me. Don't ever forget how close we are.' And I lean down to hug him, his soft, velvety fur. He says, 'Stand up. It's time to get on.' And he jumps into the sword.

"And I walk back to my spirit door. It's like I'm walking out of the inside of me with the closing of the door."

Sobbing deepy, Sue opened her eyes.

"It was like — I experienced — I could just feel everything that was between Dad and I just go. It was like he was before me, pleading with me, 'Take that, too.' He didn't know how to get close to me. He's been trying, ever since I was real little. I don't think it was him who built the wall, it was me. Because I never communicated. I always wanted him to understand where I was at, but I never asked him where he was at. Isn't it unreal that I feel all that coming out of me right now, all of a sudden it's like a picture going past me saying, 'This is why.'

"It's like I said earlier: you can't want somebody to accept you without you accepting them. It's two ways. You can't say, 'I want you to understand where I'm at but I'm not going to understand where you're at.'

"The mountain was unbelievable. It was like I could see the pain and tears, almost like the flood running out of me that I felt in different situations, wanting to be close to my dad and not understanding where I was, the confusion and loneliness and despair at not knowing what to do with myself and my life. Confusion like this big gigantic mountain with all these big rocks to step over and giant standing trees I couldn't get around, and deep warm trees, part of it growing straight, part of it growing crooked, like a big monster up there, and the snow, icy places that you might slip on and break your neck.

"It was like when the leopard put the sword in my hand I grew above it. All of a sudden I wasn't looking up at the mountain, I was looking down at it. And when I touched my sword to it, it was like — it wasn't like — it was like an explosion but it was like pieces of it, like it all went, like it exploded and then there were only pieces of it, like pieces of my past, pieces of my mind, my old feelings, my old thoughts, my old thinking, my trials. My confusion was all being blasted away.

"And then this unbelievable procession of everybody that's special in my life came before me. And each one of them had a different, was different — I gave them something different or they gave me back something different, that was in my lack of growth still, especially with my mom and dad and my son, allow him to grow, allow him to be, in other words allow him to do what your parents didn't allow you to do. I felt this, and that he has a good guide in his wife. I must let go of him and let them guide one another. And my little granddaughter, to be strong, to grow, to be happy. And....Bobby's wife had another baby, it was proven in court it wasn't his....Mary, I've never mentioned it to you, but she came before me. She's not very well taken care of and there's not very much I can do about it. She carries Bobby's name, but Bobby doesn't have custody of her, Margaret does, Bobby's ex-wife. She's been in the hospital many times with pneumonia. Strength was all I could give her. My hands are tied where she's concerned. I wish I could pluck her out of that situation and say you can't have her.

"What an exprience!. I had no idea I was going to....I wasn't even thinking of those things. It's amazing how your imagery brings all these things into something you can see and identify. That mountain was a horrible thing, a horrible part of my own life. And today it's the first day of a new beginning. It's like each day I wake up feeling stronger and stronger.

"And my leopard is such a neat animal, so powerful. I know now why he was not brought to me before I had grown. I would have feared so much power. He had so much power, so much energy. It was almost like he could point at something and make it disappear. He has so much power, almost of life and death. If I would have met him first I couldn't have handled it, he would have frightened me. And now it's like I would like to have my hand around him and I'm not afraid of him at all, even though he has all that power. He doesn't abuse his power. He's very kind, but yet in the same token, in a gentle way, if I were headed down the wrong path he would really snap me around, I would know he had done something.

"That's really neat, a neat thing to have happen."

"Sounds like a closing point, too, doesn't it?" I said.

"Yes," she said, "It's almost like they're telling me that I don't need to come very much more."

I replied, "We have another appointment set up for three weeks from now. Why don't we keep that and see where we are, and we might not have to meet after that."

"I feel strongly they have total control of my life. Which is neat. *I* have total control of my life. It's a powerful feeling. I never knew that was possible. But I do believe that they're right there. And until just a week ago I felt like I had to search them out. They're *there*. I can reach any one of them anytime I want to. Because I'm just reaching inside me."

"You also saw how big your spirit is. Bigger than the mountain," I said.

"Is that what it was? Yes, that *is* what it was. It's almost like I'd taken up the sky. How close I must've been to God at that point."

Chapter Fourteen
This is My Castle

"**I** think if I were to tell you what all has happened the last three weeks you wouldn't believe it."

"A lot has, huh?" I queried.

"Ohhh. I had an interesting situation with a friend of mine. A person I thought was a friend. I called this person up and asked them if they'd like to go to lunch, and they said no, that they had decided to divorce me from their lives, because they thought that they couldn't handle it psychologically. So we talked, for a long time.

"At first it disturbed me, and then I kind of took a walk inside myself, stepped inside my emotions and asked, 'Why is this bothering me?' Because I wasn't sure if I wanted to pick up that relationship and be a friend with this person myself, so it was kind of a testing.

"And what I found out was that this person is threatened by me and that she's the type of person that's never had a friendship. So it's 'I want to be your friend but don't tell me your problems.' A situation where I did confide in this person sometimes, when I was upset. And she resented that.

"And after working through that I came to the conclusion that I don't have the time to devote the energy to a friendship that's going to resent giving to me. And the pain went away when I realized that. There's nothing here to build this friendship on.

"If I choose to be a friend of someone, and say, 'I'll help you, I'll be your friend', I'm not going to resent that a year later, being that person's friend. She must have a lot of problems, I don't know but I think she must have a lot of problems. And I'm not going to exert any energy that way because I'm not going to get any energy back. So it's a futile effort, you just stop that and go on."

"Had you ever done that before?" I asked.

"No! I would have been hurt, 'Oh, how could this person *not* want to be my friend?!' I didn't feel those things. The thing I felt was, 'I need to find out where I'm at on this, and get rid of it, so I don't hang onto it.'

"I'm amazed at how I handled that. I'm also amazed at my positiveness. There's no negative in my life.

"Oh, I have to tell you something else that's really exciting. Did I tell you I was going to go to San Francisco?"

"To see your son?"

"Yes. He was put in the emergency room twice. He had terrible migraine headaches. Terrible. They couldn't figure out what was the matter with him. So I went down there and he was rolling on the floor in pain. I had no idea that this had been going on for about three weeks. He just couldn't stand it.

"I had sent him some of my tapes that I had for myself during biofeedback: relaxation and what not. So I went through a total relaxation with him, and I had him visualize what his pain was. He visualized a gigantic tooth, Steve.

"The next morning I took him to an emergency dental clinic, they removed a tooth, and within eight hours he had no headache and was completely rid of it. He has had no headache since. Now doesn't that just blow you away?

"I couldn't believe it. They took one ex-ray. I just took him in there and I said, 'Bobby is having problems with a tooth. I don't know where it is, but he has an abscessed tooth.' So they ex-rayed him and sure enough, he had one tooth so abscessed that he had a lesion on the gum next to this tooth, when you push on it white stuff would come out. And it was so infected, usually they don't pull a tooth during that time, that they pulled it anyway, it had to go. Put him on antibiotics and...Great!"

"Wow!"

"It blew me away. I just knew it was a tooth."

"You know the language, don't you," I said.

"It's like having the ability to step inside someone, and feel where their pain is coming from and then having some guidance into knowing what you should say. Somehow I seem to have contact with what I need to say. It's like I don't say it, like they feed me the information to know what I need to say.' When I first realized I could do that, I would kind of step inside that person, I would get hooked, and I would start fixing it, and I couldn't fix it because it wasn't my feelings, it wasn't my pain. It was very painful, it was like it would just drain me. And I don't get hooked now, whether it's my mom, or my son, I'm able to step in there, somehow get their vibrations, step out and know what it is they need to work on. No, that's going too far, *I* don't know what they need to work on. I'm able to guide them to where *they* realize what they need to work on. They naturally will flow there. It's amazing, if you can just guide them there, they, naturally, in their soul, will pick that up.

"I do have one thing that's scary to me. It's as if people become aware that there's something different about you, something deeper about you. And because you are deeper yourself, you pick up where people are really hurting.

"I have a cousin who has a young daughter, she's seventeen. About a year ago she was involved in an accident with her grandfather, he was killed, and so was his little dog. And this man who was killed is my father's brother, so I'm very close to the situation. And I haven't had much contact with my cousin, we were very close growing up. And I called her, she's the manager of Mountain Lakes Resort, and I have a sailboat that I want to sell. I thought she might have some input to where I needed to take that boat to sell it. She's very distressed. Very unhappy. She's had a lot of terrible things go on since her dad was killed in this car accident. Her daughter can't get over the fact. She's not growing. She quit growing right then. She's unable to function in school. She's almost had two complete nervous breakdowns. She has terrible dreams. Instantly, Steve, I knew what was the matter. There's something in that accident. She needs to go back to that accident and find out what it is: guilt, the tragedy of seeing her grandpa die, the grotesqueness of it, whatever it is she's hooked back there. I don't feel that I can... it's scary to me to take her back there. And I wanted to recommend to her that she bring her daughter to see you. It's too scary for me to take her there. So I wanted to ask you if it would be all right to approach her and tell her maybe she needs to contact you and maybe she could bring her daughter here. I feel it strongly. It's like I know when I shouldn't get into something. I feel that would be very scary for me.

"Not only scary, but there's a very close, personal thing also, that might be cumbersome," I said.

"It may not be scary, but I may not be able to handle what she has to say."

"It might be rough for you," I said.

"I think my total fear is.... my lack of knowledge: getting her there and her cracking or something because I didn't have the pool of knowledge to draw from to help guide her around that, or know what energy she needs to help her around it. Hey, a year ago I would have said, 'Go get 'em! We're going to do it!' But I'm so aware of other people's feelings and my own now, that I'm not going to get myself or somebody else into that situation. Too dangerous, I feel. But I did want to talk to you, so if she did call, that you would know who it is."

I replied that I would be willing to see her. I then asked Sue if she had been in touch with her animals recenlty.

"Yep. Especially my Scotty dog. My Scotty dog seems to be more separated and there's an interesting reason for that, more separated from me than my other animals. My other animals, I really don't need to be in contact with them because I am all the time. But my little Scotty dog needs that extra attention, but I didn't realize that until about a week ago, because I'm so aware of them being with me all the time without reaching out and visually seeing them, I just know they're there, because I just feel them when they do things, it's like they're saying all the time, 'Good, Sue'. I just get that feedback from them all the time coming from within.

"So I went to see my Scotty dog because I thought I'm just supposed to do it, I felt really strong about it. He wouldn't let me come near him, growling almost like he wanted to eat me up, growling and showing his teeth, so I asked him what was wrong.

"'Well, you didn't come see me. How come you haven't been to see me? I need you to come see me.'

"So I ended up picking him up and giving him lots of strokes and telling him I'm sorry. Now I'm going to see him almost every other night just to give him strokes. And I realize that... he communicated to me that all the animals are really strong except my heart. That's where he is. And that I must always be in closer contact with him, visual contact, really knowing that I'm making a contact, because my intelligence and my power and my strength and my actions are one, it's my heart that sometimes really needs lots of strength."

"It may be time for him to grow soon. Almost all the other animals have grown," I said.

"He's growing now. He's feeling better. I keep telling him that I am there, always there, but that until he feels like I don't need to do that all the time that I'll do that, because when I needed that he was always there. So I want him to know that I'm always there.

"That just blew me away when I went to see him and he's always wanted me to pick him up or hold him. He really let me know that. He said, 'Don't do this to me!' He let me know just because my strength and my intelligence is there, that's okay, he wants all these positive strokes. So that was interesting. And I think in the last week that I feel real strong that way, that I know where that's at, but it was an interesting thing to see. I feel like with my cat that I can just reach out and pet him anytime. And I can be walking along doing something I feel very positive about and I'll see a visualization of maybe my giraffe walking very elegantly across the plains, or I'll feel a nudge from my leopard saying, 'Great, that's what we're supposed to do together.' And using my thinking, I see my seagull every now and then. It's like I don't have to go into that to see that. It's like a really strong part of me is doing that, like a flash of that part of me comes to me. It's almost like... just a flash, like a flash in my mind, I'll see my seagull flying across my mind. So they're strong. But, where my Scotty dog is I still need to make a real effort to go see him. He doesn't seem to do that."

"It kind of blew me away, because the Scotty dog's never growled. And I'm getting a real strong feeling that I need to buy a Scotty dog, need to find a Scotty dog. And they're hard to find. And when you find one they're very expensive. Like three hundred dollars. And I don't have three hundred dollars to spend on a Scotty dog, so I feel that soon one is just going to appear for some reason. And I'm open to that. And

I've already covered my bases that I know I can have it and I know that when I'm supposed to have one I'll have one. And I don't know why it's so important that I have one because I've never wanted a Scotty dog, but I'm going to own one, I know that. Kind of like I need a living symbol of where I come from and where I'm going. I don't know why that is. A stuffed one won't do. So I'm just waiting for that to happen.

"I think I'd kind of like to go visit him for a little bit. Do we have time for that?"

"Well, we can run over a little," I said. "Allow yourself to breathe in that clear fresh sky and breathe away any stress or tension. And allow yourself to go to visit with your animals, particularly with your Scotty dog."

"I'm there with them. It's like the Scotty dog has got them all together. They're all just relaxing around. Scotty dog has been making a bigger effort to get to know them better. Get to know them like I know them. He was always happy to see me. He's jumped up into my arms. He said he found that as a friend of the other animals, and not just me as a friend, that he's going to be okay. He understands what I've been telling him, that I'm always there. I'm always there for them. He's really excited about that."

"See if there's aything you need to do today," I suggested.

"He said just sit with them for a little bit and kind of draw on each other's energy. They're all just really content that everything is falling into place and they're synchronizing with one another.

"The alligator says that he knows that one of the last things that I need to do was my quitting smoking and I'm going to do that this weekend. And I'm telling him that I know that.

"The leopard's asking me how I feel about the wall between my dad and I and if it's still there.

"No, it's not still there. The only thing between my dad and I is to talk, which may happen this Saturday. We're going to take my boat to San Francisco.

"My bear, she just put her arm around me like a really good friend would when you come up to them and they put their arm on your shoulder. She said it really feels good to be physically, mentally, and spiritually well. And that they will never leave me. And that they're going to work with the Scotty dog, that the last phase of my growth is almost there.

"Leopard's put his paw on me. He says that the last phases of my growth will be growing for others. That every time someone grows that I touch, that I'll grow. He said he's noticed that I haven't picked up one particle of my past since it was destroyed. And that my golden sword is sharper than ever. And that both edges are sharp and keen. That I know my limitations as well as my strengths. That I'm becoming aware of my spirit and how big it is. And that I am totally becoming in contact with myself. Total wholeness, oneness. I don't guess about what I feel anymore, I *know* what I feel. And that I'm no more afraid of hurt or pain or disappointment than I am of joy and happiness. That I have no confusion about the difference between 'I am angry' and 'I am hurt'. That was one of my biggest... he's reminding me that I haven't seen... ah, he's reminding me of something really funny. He wants me to tell you about my king cobra.

"This week my king cobra turned into a comic snake, a cartoon snake. It appeared before me like a funny cartoon. That this was the total destruction of my fear of my emotions, of being able to deal with them, and that the complete opposite is of the complete and total fear of something so horrible and dangerous to something so ridiculously funny. It was like the air went out of this cartoon snake and it just disappeared. That was one of my final growth areas. I'm telling you that it really worked. My fear of that snake really got me on the ball about working with emotions. I didn't want it to strike me. It was really horrible.

"He's handing me a puppet. The puppet looks like my cartoon snake. He says every time for the rest of my life when I come in contact with my emotions and I don't want to deal with them I'll see that puppet on my hand to remind me of how ridiculous it is.

"He says my new life and flowering and beauty has grown. And he wants me to look at it.

"And it has grown. The trees are beautiful and strong and straight. And my giraffe is there. She looks at me like she always does, and walks through the forest, picking just the right branches to nibble on. She's so elegant. So lacking in fear. Her body's just sleek. And her eyes are twinkling.

"And she has a baby by her. I didn't even know she was going to have a baby. This baby is my granddaughter, Cindy. And the leopard said that she's well protected.

"I can feel my energy, my hands are getting so warm. Like all this glow is coming over me. And as I see the more I glow around me. Leopard's showing me a flash of red. When I see red it means danger. What I fear is danger. I may see this over people. He's showing me colors and what they mean. He's saying that my sword can turn that red into light pink, which is softness, growing softer. A yellow or a whitish glow is energy, someone you can trust, someone who's filled with energy. And I must watch out for people who show a black or greyish color, or sometimes a purple glow, dark deep purple, almost black. He knows I'll work on it, and as I grow I'll see other colors and instantly I'll know what they mean. Or maybe a book. I see a book, a book I know I must read. Someone will tell me what the book is. The most important thing is to not trust people who have a cloud. That doesn't mean you can't communicate with them. You just know what your limits are with them.

"He's telling me that I will know these things without communicating with them, I'll just know them and feel them. He says people that tend to have softness have soft glows, soft colors. Their glow is easy to see, and the color is a soft color.

"My Scotty dog is curled up in my bear's arms. He says don't worry about Scotty, he's going to be fine. He says, 'It'd be good to look in on him from time to time, but he needed to learn that we're here. All of us are here. And all of us are you.'

"And it's time to form a circle, a circle of energy. And we're all in the circle. Scotty dog is in the center of the circle. And I'm given my sword. I'm touching my leopard's head and my sword's touching the Scotty dog. And my energy is circling around the Scotty dog and he disappears into my sword.

"And I see an energy glow around us in the circle. And my sword's in the center of the circle, touching the center of the circle. And it's like they're fading into me, into my sword, into me. And as my leopard gets to the sword he's telling me I will always be there, I will always have my double-edged sword. And that I'll only have to look as far as myself to be with them: all of them or any one of them.

"They're gone now, and I'm looking at the forest I've created. As I look around it's so full of strengths. There's nothing scary about it. It just grows in strength. Eveything around it is alive and green and beautiful.

"There's a house. And I walk in the door of the house.

144

The house is full of gold walls, and... it looks a lot like a castle for kings. This is *my* castle. This is my world. And I can have anything in it I want. It's like when I open the door of my house I see the whole world, even it's ugliness and beauty.

"Now it's time for me to leave."

Sue gently opened her eyes. "My world's really a neat place, now."

"Very rich, " I replied.

"It really is. I wish I could take a picture and show you all the beauty there."

"Why don't you draw it someday," I suggested.

"That would be neat."

Chapter Fifteen
The Process

The reader may feel that my interaction with Sue during our sessions was minimal. It was. Particularly during the latter sessions I said little. My main function was to help Sue enter a state of relaxation and to begin her meeting with the animals. From there on she and they essentially took over. There was litle need for me to say much. Sue was beautifully attentive to her imagery and deeply respected her animals. There was also a deep trust between us, so it made my part easy. But this is not the case with every client.

My initial function is obviously to introduce the client to the animals. For someone who is already practiced in imagery a simple way is to say to them: "let an animal come out of your head (or throat, heart, solar plexus, belly, feet/legs/pelvis or let one appear at the top of your head) and just watch to see what it is.

For someone who has had no prior experience with guided imagery I first take them through the visualization of a seed in the earth which begins to grow as they watch it. Then I have them interact with it, asking what it has to tell them, what it needs from them, whether it will help them grow, etc. This is helpful in that it allows the imagery to develop slowly and naturally, paving the way for more complex imagery and interaction. Occasionally the plant or tree that grew will subsequently show up in the imagery with their chakra animals.

I then have them focus one by one in the different chakra areas, experiencing the feelings that are there and then allowing an animal to emerge from that area while they watch. Good communication is vital during this time as sometimes something other than an animal appears and that is what they need to work with. Whatever image appears is the valid image. At the beginning of the work I always suggest to them that the imagery itself knows why it is there and our job is just to observe it and learn and grow from it.

Occasionally I have asked the client to allow the feelings that are in the chakra area to turn themselves into an animal and this appears to be just as valid a procedure.

Then on subsequent occasions, after the animals have been intially contacted, I merely suggest to the individual that they go to meet with their particular animal, either naming it in terms of the animal itself or in terms of the chakra location (grounding animal, gut animal, etc.). If the council has previously been formed I will open the session by suggesting to the person that they go to meet with their animals wherever they may be and to tell me which one they first encounter. This allows the animals to emerge in the sequence that is most suitable to them on that particular occasion. Of course every session is preceded by suggestions of relaxation.

People who have done much personal growth work, or who have had a lot of prior therapy, or who are artistic or imaginative, or who are very hungry to grow are usually immediately able to see the significance of the animals in their lives.

Sometimes the initial meeting is a deeply heartfelt one, the animals saying something like, "You've finally come to meet me! I've waited for you for such a long time!"

But sometimes the animals may be disdainful, hostile, hurt, angry, injured, bound, tethered, or caged in some way. In this case my task is to help the client begin a healing relationship with the animal and to learn to treat it with respect, exploring the nature of it's circumstances and what needs to be done in order to enable it to be free and healthy. Sometimes this involves a personal experience between the animal and the client and sometimes it requires the entire council to be involved. In either case we need to insure that the injury is not exacerbated or perpetuated.

The fundamental way to do this is to help them get to know each other better: initially through dialogue and interaction, asking the client to see what the animal has to tell him/her, and asking the animal if there is anything it needs or if there is anything the client can do for it. I then encourage the client to provide immediately whatever the animal needs rather than only understanding it metaphorically. IT IS ALL RIGHT TO UNDERSTAND IT METAPHORICALLY BUT THE ANIMAL NEEDS ALSO TO BE RELATED TO IN THE IMMEDIACY OF ITS EXISTENCE, NOT MERELY AS IF IT WERE A MESSAGE "ABOUT". To treat it as if it were only a metaphor about other aspects of one's life is to miss the fact that it is also the nucleus of the connection to those other aspects. So it is the prime place to begin those changes in oneself and that respect for the totality of one's Being which need to be engendered. It is surprising how healing this can be, and it becomes so evident that most people have not specifically attended to particular aspects of themselves for many years. Occasionally this initial contact in itself is adequate to initiate a change or transformation in the animal and the client.

A subsequent step, done at a later session, is having the client become the animal. This is undertaken only with the consent of both the animal and the client, for it is never a matter of demanding or intruding upon an animal, but of respecting it. It is seldom that an animal refuses to allow the person to become it, and just as seldom that the client refuses to become a particular animal. But there are some situations in which this does occur, and also situations in which I intuitively feel it inadvisable to have the client become the animal.

Becoming the animal always seems to open up a new dimension of the clients understanding. I initiate this by asking the client to merge into the animal, taking on it's characteristics, seeing through it's eyes, hearing through it's ears, smelling through it's nose, feeling through it's skin, experiencing it's emotions, attitudes, orientation, thoughts, interests, etc. And also particularly asking the person to experience the animal moving, running, flying, resting; to feel it's power and it's relationship with the world in which it lives. I then ask the client to tell me what most stands out about this experience.

Upon doing this the client frequently begins to experience his/her aliveness much more profoundly, and one can see a bristling of energy, or an enriched ruddiness to the skin of the face, or the experience of some deep emotion. The client also gains an appreciation for how distinct and individual the animals are, and also for the clarity of their existence: they don't wobble; they just are who they are in full sincerity and not without a touch of humor. One client said to me, "They seem more human than most humans."

In this one also gains an overall view of the dynamics of the individual. What elements of him/her self has the client most identified with: which of the animals feels most "like" the client? Which are most remote from the client? Which are restrained? Which have developed powerfully?

In one interesting individual who was gay the heart animal was missing: there was only a deep cave that had been long abandoned. The power animal was a spider with an elephant's nose, looking like Ganesh. The grounding animal was a stallion that was always hazy and indistinct. The client felt most like the spider, always scheming and spinning webs. In our work we discovered that the heart animal had originally been an elephant that had been devoured by the spider power animal when the client was hurt in a love relationship. The devouring was for protective reasons but it had also kept the client from being involved in any other serious relationships. When he was finally able to get close to his grounding stallion he found that it was extremely powerful and highly masculine. He was surprised to find how friendly and supportive it was, and as he rode it he had deep memories of his childhood relationship with his father and how hurt and angry he had been when his father began favoring a new little sister. Upon becoming the stallion he experienced it's powerful masculinity and his sexual interest in women began to awaken.

In another individual the heart animal was a rat. He was rather horrified at this and said "I don't like rats!" But as he got to know the rat, and particularly upon becoming it, he began to realize other qualities of the rat: that it was a survivor, that when cornered it would fight for it's survival with an intense fury, and that it never deliberately hurt anyone else. This gave him a whole new perspective on both the history and the nature of his rat and he began to value it much more.

As the clients relation to the animal changes, the animal itself changes. It may grow in size, it may become healed or stronger or brighter or more distinct. Or it may become transformed into a totally different animal. And as the animal changes the client changes.

By far the most difficult part of my work is with people who tend to intrude into and interfere with the process of their own growing. The standard way of doing this has cultural roots: the negating, belittling, and discounting of the imaginal process itself. It is difficult for the person to understand that in doing this he/she is negating, belittling, and discounting him/herself! But sometimes that is exactly the nature that it assumes: "I don't like myself! I always make mistakes! I never do the right thing!," etc. What this does is to keep intact a logical or rational accounting of their own supposed identity, whether positive or negative, but it does so by denying them the fullness, richness, and creativity that is their natural heritage.

One facet of this mode of interfering is to see the animals only metaphorically, only in terms of what they "mean". What this does is to say that they have value only when translated into how they fit into the conceptual, similar to valuing a foreign language only in its translation into English, rather than learning the experience and the value of the language itself, including all of its untranslatable aspects and it's relationship to it's originating culture.

Sometimes the interfering can be overcome by adressing the interfering process directly. Expressing appreciation to it for its obvious positive qualities, for its usefulness in the survival of the individual in this particular culture, for its dedication to the support of the individual, etc., for even the self-negating individual has apparently copied what someone else did to them at one time, lessening the hurt by beating them to the punch. And then to tell it that at this time something more, something other, needs to be accomplished. Now the individual is involved in growing toward original wholeness rather than in just meeting the demands imposed by survival in a particular familial, social or educational role, and that support is now needed in this new direction.

One easy and initial form of support that the intruder can provide is to request of it that it frequently ask the question, "How can I grow from this?" Asking this question is perhaps one of the most significant activities it can learn to perform. What this does is to focus one's awareness on the positive outcome of whatever situation the person is in. Even if a seemingly disastrous event has occurred, to ask this question brings a person to focus on and enter a process which draws from the event whatever positive features it might have in one's own evolution, thus using it as a stepping stone in one's growing.

But we must also know how to deal with questions. Many of us have learned to jump for an answer as soon as a question is asked, and I have even known people who use questions themselves as an intrusive device, asking things like, "What good will this do?" or, "How do I know that will do any good?", etc., so that they use the question itself to close off potential avenues of development. The natural function of a question is to open up potentialities, possibilities: *ask the question and then hold open a conscious space into which the answer can come of it's own accord.* Don't try to force or manufacture the answer. Allow the question to be a true questing.

Many of us have been taught that the thinking intellect is supposed to do it all. But if it assumes that responsibility then it is bound to become weighted down and tremendously frustrated, because it is attempting to do things that are not within it's rightful domain. One afternoon a man called me in tremendous distress. His wife had left him two weeks before, taken their two children, and gone to live with her mother. He had an intense headache and didn't know which way to turn. The first thing I did was to get in touch with his heart animal because I thought that's where the greatest disturbance would be. I was surprised to see that his heart animal was a deer, calmly nibbling at grass in a forest. So I got in touch with his power animal: it also was calm and undisturbed, and each subsequent animal was found to be calm and at ease until we came to his head animal. It was an octopus and it's tentacles were aching from being stretched to the limit by trying to hold everything together. We told it that it didn't have to do everything itself and praised it for having been willing to take on such a tremendous task. We then asked if it would allow the other animals to help it and in great relief it agreed. The other animals came willingly forth, the octopus let go of what it was trying to hold onto, and the man's headache abruptly ceased.

In a similar way sometimes the interfering process can be shown its limiting nature. In one individual when two animals merged they became an egg. The shell of the egg was quite tough and the egg could not hatch. When the session ended this person told me that he was very aware that he had just been creating all the imagery himself and that therefore it was worthless. I asked him if that was the case then why was it that he had been unable to hatch the egg. He had no answer for this. When he arrived for our next session a week later he told me that my statement had made him aware of how he discounts processes of imagination and feeling within himself that cannot be accounted for logically, and he was much more open to pursuing the visualizations. When the egg finally did hatch, some sessions later, inside was a terrified two-year old boy, himself.

Sometimes the self-interfering extends all the way to the inception of imagery. I have had several clients who claimed to have no imagery, but upon close inspection it was discovered that the imagery presented itself but was quickly discounted before it could be fully formed. For example, a person may begin by seeing only the ear of an animal and discount it because it is not the total animal. One client was able to overcome this, and then much later, to our surprise, her imagery suddenly began appearing in color.

There are other reasons, though, why no visual imagery may appear: the person's main mode of imaging may be auditory or kinesthetic. The person may need to listen for the animal, or to feel the animal, rather than trying to see it.

We can recognize the intrusive process most readily when it is bizarre or out of context, as in the obsessive individual, for example. But we have characteristically failed to recognize it as destructively intrusive when it takes on the character of logic and reasoning. These people, and usually those around them, are quite unaware of their intrusiveness into their own process because it is done in a logical way. They usually feel that the only events with any validity are those that conform to rational logic. Work with these people is initially quite tedious because they are used to generating a logical response to everything rather than observing and allowing themselves to learn and grow. Their learned need for logic, rather than wholeness, is itself the destructive element.

These are all problems of awareness. The client is unable to observe the contents of their awareness without immediately commenting on, criticizing, rejecting, or in some way reacting to some aspect of it. It is this intrusive reactivity that is the fundamental problem. And sometimes the process of self-interfering is so pervasive that the client does not allow the time necessary for its resolution before terminating therapy.

Interestingly, the self-interfering act frequently shows

up in the imagery itself once the imagery has been allowed time to manifest: a destructive teenager that barges in and throws the ongoing imagery into chaos, a bloody knife that suddenly appears and cuts a brain in half, a disembodied voice that at significant moments comments on the meaninglessness of the ongoing imagery, etc.

The natural and original orientation of the animals, and ourselves, is to function in harmonious interrelationship, and it is this energy that I am most in touch with during a therapy session, recognizing that the self-intrusive process is a surface variation which came about usually as a means of surviving in an earlier limiting environment. The self-interfering response was learned and now perseveres as a generalized survival response except that now it limits ones growth. This situation leads to a division between aspects of who we are and it is that division that needs to be healed. Whatever maintains that division will need to voluntarily bring itself to an end, which it does by learning once again to trust the orientation which arises from it's original wholeness.

Meeting and becoming the animals begins the process of integration. But a major step in integration begins with the creation of the council. I do this by having the client contact the Crown animal first and asking if this would be a good time for the animals to meet in council, and we then follow the Crown animal's advice. If the Crown animal indicates that it is not appropriate for the council to gather, some other growing at a more specific level probably needs to occur first. I also have the client ask if the Crown animal will help in gathering the animals together. Usually they gather readily, but occasionally one is reluctant or resistant to joining the council. This is then treated as a matter that needs to be dealt with in council, not by trying to coerce the animal.

The client is asked to observe any conflicts, animosities, friendships, or groupings that occur as the animals gather. I then suggest that the client ask if they will gather into a circle, which they usually have done already, and to address them as a council. the client is free to say anything to them he/she wants, but there are also certain topics I suggest: to express his/her appreciation for their willingness to gather together, to express hope that they will be willing to resolve any conflicts between them, to appreciate their differences, to support each other, and to live harmoniously. I also suggest that the client ask them for their support in his/her own growth and offer them his or her own support in their growth. If no topic emerges spontaneously, I have the client ask that the animals consult among themselves and see if there is any consensus as to what the first order of business should be.

From here on my task is usually to observe and insure that all animals have a chance to be heard. If the client tells me that the animals say a certain one of them needs to grow, for example, I ask the client to ask that particular animal if it is ready to grow, if it knows how to do this, etc. I prefer for the direction to come from the animals as soon as possible, and as little as necessary from me. I see my task as that of helping the client move toward being in touch with their own process and of learning to trust and allow it.

Frequently during the imagery when a person says something to me about an animal I ask them to repeat it to the animal itself. My function is not to have them create a dialog with me, but to help them begin to stitch together an internal communication, an inner communion, opening up little rivulets which in time can become great rivers. Our fundamental problem is, after all, that we have lost the connection with different parts of who we are, through rejection, distancing, remoteness, insulation, interfering, or any of the other psychological terms that have come to be used in this regard: repression, compartmentalization, etc. Our great need is for all parts of who we are to be in full and open communion with all other parts, so that we can act from a center that is in contact and harmony with our totality. And when we act that we ultimately support who we are and feel supported by who we are.

And this is not to be confused with control. It is not that one part of us is intended to control other parts, as we may have been taught: that our thinking or language or logic is to be in control. But that all parts are open to sharing Being. Our center can only be true when all parts are fully present and in balance. And work with the inner animals is a major way to regain this.

One of the most difficult things to learn is to stay out of the picture when everything is going smoothly. We not only have difficulty learning this with respect to ourselves, but as therapists working with clients as well: to allow the client their own imagery, not to intrude with one's own. And to give them sufficient space. When a client is silent for a long period I will ask, "What's happening now?", not in a demanding but in a gently inquisitive way. In working with groups, where one doesn't have the immediate verbal feedback from each individual, there are long periods of silence and it takes some experience with the process to realize that much is going on and to allow it adequate time to occur.

The imagery has it's own dynamics and it's own point of completion, it's own closure; it brings itself to it's own appropriate ending. For this reason it is difficult to work within the schedule of a fifty minute hour when using deep imagery. The organic time unit is generally much closer to the dream cycle, approximately ninety minutes. And like the dream cycle it varies from person to person.

The Totem Pole process is stunning in the constantly progressive changes that are observed from one session to the next. The animals seem to know the optimum pacing of experiences that result in growth, and the necessary sequence. This in itself results in a thoroughness of growth which requires the shortest amount of time. My work with Sue took place in 15 sessions. This is remarkable, especially considering the fact that she had essentially given up on traditional therapies of which she had experienced numerous varieties. Early in our therapy she told me that she was amazed that the changes were occurring with no effort, since every previous type of therapy she had undergone seemed to have demanded tremendous effort and resulted in very litle change.

It is evident, however, that her earlier therapies had not dealt with, adequately, at least, the foundational issues of her difficulties. And yet the animals went immediately to those issues, without my being aware, prior to the fact, that they even existed. But it should certainly be acknowledged that an essential element was Sue's deep and earnest desire to grow, the seriousness of her commitment, and the quality of her attention.

No verbal description can adequately portray the aliveness, the immediacy, and the direct emotional engagement which the Totem Pole process allows the client. Each animal has its own unique personality, and the animals, both individually and collectively, rapidly evolve into a valued inner support system. Natural leaders appear among them whose wisdom and understanding are tacitly honored by the others. As the animals go through their own growth and transformation the leadership may shift. I have encountered a few situations where at the beginning of the work one animal may attempt to impose its domination over the others but the others have responded as if this were an immature attitude, and the animal was soon willing to grow beyond it. And although there may occasionally be initial animosity between some of the animals, a cooperation, respect, trust and support emerge among them as they get to know one another and engage in common projects.

The Totem Pole process is also valuable in that it bypasses the rut of intellection, explaining, accounting for, and describing everything in one's life. One client who had been to several other therapists was shocked when I told her that there was no real need to replay the sequence of her life's problems for me, an approach in which she was apparently well practiced. It also circumvents the ego defense system as nothing from without is brought in to the clients ego, but instead it is as if the ego engages other elements of the clients Being. It is essential, however, that the client be willing to *allow* the imagery rather than attempting to control it.

The factor of allowing the imagery is a point which I feel requires serious attention. Most popular books on visualization involve what I call "canned" imagery, i.e., one imagines one's desires as already being fulfilled and concentrates on this imagery. This is essentially the perpetuation of an ego attitude through the use of controlled imagery, and in my experience little *fundamental* change can occur. On the other hand, in imagery which is *allowed,* what I call "deep" imagery, elements that are beyond the ego are allowed to help the ego grow beyond its usual boundaries, into that interrelationship with Being on Being's terms, not on the ego's terms.

As well as promoting growth and balance, this process also allows a continuity over time which provides an ongoing assessment of the status of the client. I have done sessions with some individuals who are very advanced in their own growth work and they have been both fascinated to observe their own status as well as pleased to be shown the areas in which further work is needed, in a remarkably systematic way. It also provides the therapist with a valuable source for assessing the appropriateness of intervention and the proper pacing of the therapy. And it simultaneously provides the support of the clients strengths as well as focussing on the problem areas.

Although the esthetic simplicity of this approach makes it appear that it could readily be used as a popular technique, it is essential that the therapist be aware, sensitive, and completely respecting of the client. This is definitely not a matter of intruding or of imposing ones own sense of where the client should be, but a matter of trusting those elements within the client which know, like seeds, where and at what rate the growth needs to occur.

There are certain precautions that I always give my clients. One is to refrain from actively engaging in visualizing the animals between sessions, but if they should appear spontaneously to ask why they have come. Later, as therapy progresses, the animals themselves can be asked about the appropriateness of the client contacting them on his/her own, and sometimes the animals themselves raise this issue. The most important precaution, however, is to always respect the animals.

The importance of this was made vitally clear by an early client who would actively visualize her animals between our regular sessions where she made demands on them and tried to force them to do things. They quickly became passive and unresponsive and she, in turn, became flat and depressed. They didn't become active again until she apologized to them and began treating them with respect, and then her depression lifted immediately.

The animals participation is to be requested, never demanded; and they, in turn, advise but do not impose. The therapist should be aware that the client is allowing him into an inner world where respect and sensitivity are valued, and where cooperation is the fundamental orientation.

Working with the animals has shown me with intimate precision the unique individuality of every person that I have worked with. It has become very evident in using this work that no two people are alike. Furthermore, it is evident that the person was created to live in a natural inner harmony, with all elements living in cooperation with one another, and growth being allowed and respected.

However, I have been able to make some generalizations about some of the animals. These generalizations are necessarily brief and limited because by far my overall experience at all levels has been to marvel at the remarkable *variety* of animals and situations that appear.

The Crown or Spiritual animal is frequently a bird or a flying animal and the client usually experiences a deep peacefulness in its presence. It is usually expressive of a deep wisdom and the other animals regard it with respect. Frequently the Crown animal plays the part of an observer, overviewing the situation without participating directly. For instance, when the council circle of animals was formed one client reported that the Crown animal, an eagle, was outside the circle perched nearby on the branch of a tree. Another said that his Crown animal, a hawk, flew high above the council, in view of the other animals and aware of them, but apparently with a wider perspective. Still a third reported that when his animals engaged in a dance, the crown animal, an owl, stood to one side, observing but not participating. With another client, however, whose Crown animal was an eagle circling high in the sky when first encountered, it told her that it was flying too high and needed to come down and be closer to the other animals. However much of a non-participant stance the Crown animal assumes, it *is* capable of direct and immediate action when this is needed.

The Head animal (Intellectual/Intuitive) initially appears in two primary modes: as an animal that is quite grown and capable, or as an animal that is underdeveloped or hidden, protective. I feel this results from our educational system which prizes intellectual learning and essentially imposes on us for years throughout our early life the need to survive in a system in which we are valued or devalued in regard to our intellectual abilities. Occasionally two animals will be present: two bear cubs, male and female; a wolf and a coyote; etc. Initially I suggest that the client ask if they are willing to merge together and if it becomes evident that the two should not merge I then assume that they are representative of both the intellect and the intuition.

The Throat animal (Communication) is frequently the least evolved of the animals: a caterpillar, snake, mouse, etc. This is probably the result of living in a culture that does not really help a child learn to communicate, perhaps through a misunderstanding of what communication is, but most likely resulting from the theoretical perspective that children need to be trained or molded in order to be who they are. In my view this is totally wrong, and an orientation that damages the child by negating the beauty of his/her subjectivity. *The function of communication is to lend open expression to one's experience:* words, language, expression, should be available to all aspects of who we are, so that every part can gain vocal expression. Instead we teach the child to fear being wrong, to fear expressing something because that expression has been punished in the past, to speak only that which would be approved, etc.

It is in the transformation of the throat animal that one experiences the startling immediacy of the effects of this work. One client who had a tight and constrained voice had a mouse as her throat animal. It lived in a small hole in the wall. When she asked what it needed it told her that it's hole was too small and asked if she could make it bigger. She was able to stretch the hole to a larger size that was more comfortable for the mouse. Immediately her voice became fuller and deeper.

The Heart animal (Love/Compassion) appears as a lion, bear, dove, etc., expressions of beautiful and powerful compassion. Or it may be recessive, retreating, fearful of being hurt (having obviously been hurt before): a bird with a broken wing, a sensitive and elusive deer, etc. the heart animal frequently plays a major role among the animals and in the circumstances of one's life.

The Solar Plexus animal (Power) is sometimes quite magnificent, sometimes held in, sometimes feared, and in women it is frequently underdeveloped. I understand this to result from living in a culture that does not have a clear and open view about power. A culture that sees power primarily in terms of control, coercion, imposition, domination, rather than understanding power as the capacity to be fully present and to act with precision, directness and clarity. Women occasionally express the fear that if they allow their power animal to grow they will become overly masculine, yet when the growing does ultimately occur what emerges in them is a deep, warm, powerful, nurturing feminine quality.

The Gut animal (Emotion) is occasionally a large or wild animal that is restrained in some way, by being caged or confined. It's release is occasionally feared by the person, and then the person is surprised to discover that it is not dangerous once released and that it's apparent ferociousness was the *result* of being confined. Or it may be a bear just emerging from hibernation. The most frequently appearing animal, however, is a dolphin, indicative of playfulness, fluidity, capable of diving to great depths or leaping into the air, being friendly and supportive.

The Grounding animal (feet, legs, pelvis) is frequently either substantial or inadequately grown. Usually in it's growth the person recalls emotional episodes from childhood that had never been resolved. When grown it is usually strong, solid, or agile, and frequently has a very close relationship with the Crown animal. Horses and giraffes appear frequently in this position.

Several other general aspects of this work need to be mentioned as well. One involves transformation. Sometimes transformations take place by the animal just changing and perhaps going through several intermediate stages before it stabilizes in its new form. Occasionally the animal will just disappear or leave, requiring the client to face and deal with issues of loss and letting go. It may also go through a formal death and burial, with the new animal subsequently appearing. It may even dissolve into the earth with the new animal then growing out of the earth.

Transformation also occasionally happens with the old

animal being eaten by the new animal and the qualities of the former becoming expanded or amplified into the larger form. The similarity to Native American tales of transformation through ingestion is quite interesting (Storm, 1973). However, this is to be differentiated from instances where one chakra animal eats another as a means of taking control over the other, and whose end result is a limitation rather than an expansion.

Interestingly, both of these aspects of ingestion appeared in a beautifully moving series of visualziations. A woman in her forties who lives in the Southwest encountered, as her Crown animal, a tarantula named Magna. She did not understand the tarantula and would not accept it, so her head animal, an eagle, ate it.

At a later session the tarantula again appeared. On this occasion she was more able to accept it and spent some time getting to know it, even becoming it so she could experience what it was like living as a spider.

At the next session the woman asked the animals if they would help her to become more accepting. She stood in the center of their circle and asked all the animals to shine their light on her. Each one produced a beam of light emanating from its heart and they illuminated her. She reported, "As they focused their energy on me I felt extremely light and uplifted--filled with strength and happiness."

When she next met with the animals the tarantula was not present but a small desert owl was seated on a branch beside her head eagle. As they formed the council, which met in a meadow, the owl did not join them. As she later described the meeting, "My power animal was a large, old buck with huge, heavy antlers weighing down his head. I could feel his aching arthritic bones and joints. His coat was covered with old scars. His name was Cary, both for 'caring' and for 'carrying.' I ask Cary what his scars are. He says they are all the hurts and things I cannot let go of. I ask what we can do to heal them and he says he wants us to shine our light on him. He goes to the center of the circle and we all direct our energy at him. He looks so tired, his head so heavy. As he stands there in the golden glow of our directed energy, he begins to look younger: strong, serene, his coat has become sleek, the scars have disappeared. His joints had been arthritic, his bones brittle; I feel them growing strong and firm, the ache leaving his joints. His horns grow light, like golden filigree. His hooves are sparkling. I go to him and put my arms around his neck. He is very affectionate, gentle and caring, but he asks me to go back to my place and to shine our light upon him again. I do that and our energy becomes a golden dust devil swirling around Cary. He becomes an indistinct shape within it. The glow begins to dissipate. All the other animals are looking anticipatory. At first I think no one is there as the light fades and then I notice a tiny spotted fawn, newborn, just struggling to his feet. All the animals welcome him. The Kangaroo (the gut animal) wants to put the fawn in her pouch. I ask the fawn if it is Cary and it says, "Yes, but my name is now Carrie." Carrie is a female deer. She is now walking better, and the owl flies down from the tree and sits on Carrie's back. I ask the owl what she represents. She says she is the Knowledge that Cary needed in order to change, knowledge that I could let go of the hurts. She says this is all part of acceptance. She says, 'Acceptance is the process and the process is acceptance.'

"Then she and Carrie enter the whale's mouth (the whale is her heart animal). The owl says they need to spend time with the whale and that the rest of us can come or stay as we wish. The kangaroo and lioness (grounding animal) go with Carrie and the owl. I stay in the meadow with Abel (the eagle head animal) and Amelia (the hawk communications animal) who groom each other.

"After a time, the whale's mouth opens and the kangaroo, Carrie, who is much bigger now, and the owl, all riding on the head of the lioness, emerge. The owl tells me that the lioness needs her now.

"I finally realize the tarantula is not there. I ask the animals if they know where Magna is. The owl says she ate her. She says she is not Abel's kind of knowledge. She is the spiritual knowledge that Magna had plus the warmth and acceptance of the desert. The rain, sun, flash floods, dust devils, and solitude were added to Magna's mystery and became something more, 'Summa cum Beauty, that's what spirituality is.' She stays with the lioness who she says was too concerned with hunting and caring for her young and who needs to be more accepting."

On several different occasions the Crown or the head animal has said that it's basic nature is that of transformation. In one young man the Crown animal was a figure that he came to refer to as the "Chameleon Man". It had the property of appearing in the form of any animal whatsoever, including that of a man. It informed my client that its primary property was Change or Transformation, and its job was to teach him about this dimension in his own life.

When I first began working with this man his throat animal appeared as three geese and a hawk. The geese were constantly arguing with each other so that it was difficult for much else to go on. I had him ask these four animals if they would be willing to merge together. The hawk was willing but the geese weren't. However in the next session the three geese had already merged into one goose, but it was still opposed to merging with the hawk. In fact, the goose was the most oppositional of all the animals. It was constantly the center of attention and usually at odds with all the other animals. On each subsequent session I would have my client ask the goose if it was willing to merge with the hawk, but still it would not.

Then at the beginning of one session my client told me about a ski trip from which he had just returned. He described how he had become aware while climbing a hill that the goose had been constantly present, cautioning him or warning him of dangers along the way. He told me he had realized the goose was only trying to be helpful but in doing so it was intrusive and distracting. I asked my client who the voice reminded him of and he immediately replied "My mother!"

In our visualization I asked him to thank the goose for being so concerned about his welfare and for protecting him when he was young, but also to explain to the goose that now he was much older and no longer needed such continued protectiveness. He also told the goose that he needed it to be with him in a much more valuable capacity now, as someone who could remind him of the need to grow, especially in circumstances that were difficult. The goose was only too happy to take on this new assignment.

The goose then agreed to merge with the hawk but both the goose and the hawk said they didn't know how to go about merging. At this point the Chameleon Man abruptly stepped forth and said, "Here, I know how to handle this. Goose, you and Hawk stand here facing me. Now both of you close your eyes. Goose, you take two steps to the left, and Hawk, you take two steps to the right." As they did this the two animals were experienced as superimposed on each other. Chameleon Man then told them to open their eyes. They did so and were confused as to their identity upon which they suddenly became an owl. Owl turned out to be settled, aware, and wise, and my clients overprotective "conscience" ceased being so bothersome.

The setting in which the council meets appears to be highly significant. Frequently there is concern on the part of the client that the setting be capable of accomodating all of the animals, those that live in the sea as well as those on land and air. In one young lady who had held herself rather rigidly closed and socially conforming for most of her life the council met for the first two times in a cave, their next meeting was under water in the sea, and ultimately they met in an open plain. This was accompanied by her gradual acknowledgement and allowing of more and more of her own individuality to be present.

The council also has a close relationship with the terrain: the trees, mountains, sun, sky, etc. Frequently they will meet around a central fire. A significant event in their meeting is celebration. Sometimes when some siginificant growth has occurred they will spontaneously celebrate by dancing in a circle around the fire, sometimes gaining such momentum that their individuality is blurred and they appear to the client as a single unified energy.

Occasionally the chakra image appears as something other than an animal, even though clients are specifically asked to allow it to appear as an animal. This has happened at the Crown chakra more frequently than at any of the other chakra sites. My own Crown "animal" has been a cylindrical shaft of golden sunlight which sometimes illuminates the other animals, engulfing them with a golden glow. With another the

Crown animal has appeared as a cluster of stars in the sky that are capable of communication, of directed illumination through a beam of light, and of causing beams of light to emanate from various chakra positions in the client. With others it has appeared as a triangle, a lotus blossom, an angel, Jesus Christ, and the sky. In one particular individual it began as a pair of Clydesdale horses who then turned into two spirits in human form, one very large and the other the same size as the client, and who were referred to by the client as the "God creatures".

Other non-animal elements that have appeared at the chakra sites are a diamond at the head chakra, a crystal at the throat, a Buddha at the heart, a ray of sun, ice crystals, or the sea at the solar plexus, a tree in the gut, or the earth or a flower in the grounding area. It must be emphasized, however, that these non-animal elements appear in only a very small percentage of cases.

What the animals have shown us is that our growth and evolution are controlled by factors deep within. What one discovers in therapy is that this natural growth has been interfered with, either by circumstances or by our own interference through attempts to control. It is evident that we need to re-learn how to support, nurture, and trust this inner process.

Any culture worthy of perpetuation should have as it's pinnacle the nurturing of human growth, nurturing it to it's fullest. Not the inculcation of beliefs or behaviors, not the conditioning of responses, not the perpetuation of a form of government, not the development of forms of commerce, although these might be adjunctive processes. If we were to truly understand the significance of the animals, and give them their due respect, humanity could undergo it's own transformation in one generation.

Thre are some who may have trouble thinking about what I have described here, but that is one of the difficulties with thinking: there are aspects of who we are that are far from the domain of thinking, and the only way we can know about them is through experience. Thinking has a difficult time trying to portray them in language either for ourselves or others; language just does not lend itself well to some of these other dimensions. And that is not to fault language, but just to describe the situation as it is. We live in a culture that functions so concentratedly in thought and language that those aspects of ourselves that do not lend themselves well to these articulations tend eventually to go ignored, except in some pockets of people.

To be completely in touch with who we are we have to, in some aspects, go beyond thought and language. And this can be greatly facilitated by the chakra animals: they are pathways to those elements and experiences that can fill out our Being.

Postscript

In 1982 when Teresa Rennick and I were in the final stages of completing our book Inner Journeys we founded the Institute for Visualization Research (IVR), along with my wife, Kay. It is a non-profit organization dedicated to research and communication in the use of imagery as a health and growth promoting process.

We felt at the time, and even more so now, that imagery was the emergent process in our culture and that it would soon be the process of primary application in therapy and the healing arts. Inner Journeys was written from the need to portray imagery as itself foundational, i.e., not reducible to intellectual meaning. This was before the chakra animals had been discovered. I now see imagery to be ultimatly emerging as the process around which our education and our future culture needs to be woven if we are to regain our connection with that core of personal undersanding and integrity that has long been absent.

A number of things have been happening in our culture. Emerging from an almost militarily lockstep conformism we have come to acknowledge, sometimes gradually and sometimes in great spurts, the fundamental need for individual growth and responsibility. Along with this has come an interest in therapy.

Thirty years ago therapy was viewed as the last resort. Today it is a handy pathway. Large numbers of people are interested in becoming therapists. What this says to me is that large numbers of people see as their primary function that of helping others grow. Growth, both physical, psychological, and spiritual is a natural process that will proceed from the inside out and is itself fulfilled when no traumatic or intrusive events occur which cause it to adhere to that event. Therapy helps the adhesion to heal so growing can continue. Growing also cannot proceed naturally without the full inclusion of our totality, all parts of who we are. Guided imagery in general, and the Personal Totem Pole process in particular, help bring this totality to bear so that healing and growth can occur most fully.

We are interested in establishing IVR as a research and training institute to explore new areas in imagery and to train those who are intrested in using imagery in their work, whether they are therapists, healers, educators, artists, businessmen, or just interested people. We are currently exploring different resources that can help this come about.

We have also been engaged in various projects, either current or proposed, concerned with the exploration and use of imagery.

For the past two years Teresa and Barbara Oglesby have been running a pilot program on the use of the Personal Totem Pole Process in counseling with Native Americans. This work continues and is expected to grow.

In my own work with Sue the hand animals were significant to her process. Whether or not this would have been the case had we begun with the core animals is difficult to say. There have been other situations where the hand animals illuminated aspects of the person's situation that had not yet been dealt with by the core animals. My own feeling is that the pertinent issues would have eventually surfaced and that the hand animals accelerated this by bringing in more aspects of the individual.

In a minor way, with one group I also explored foot animals, and again, their existence seems full of potential.

From these I then began to explore an animal for the right and left halves of the body which proved quite interesting. I presented a workshop on this at the anuual conference of the Association for Transpersonal Psychology in 1985. Subsequently, Dianne Timberlake explored the relationship between the right and left side animals and performance on the Myers-Briggs test in her Master's paper at John F. Kennedy University.

I have also done some work with animals representative of other polarities: the dorsal and ventral halves (i.e., front and back), the upper and lower halves, and the inner and outer halves, with powerful results.

Lisa Dickson and Mel Bucholtz, without knowledge of each other, have explored animals from impaired body organs with excellent results.

I have recently begun work with animals in the senses (eyes, ears, etc.) and with animals for the four modes of knowing. This work will be presented in a subsequent publication.

Another fascinating area that is being explored employs the chakra animals in couples work. First each person is individually helped to contact their animals and form the council. The two people are then brought together and a simultaneous visualization is conducted in which their chakra animals at each level are allowed to interact and the relationship between these animals is explored. This provides an immediate view of the nature of the relationship: areas of conflict and the nature of the conflict, areas where there may be little contact, and also areas where the relationship is sound and healthy. It is also possible to work at each of these levels on improving the relationship.

People also have cross-chakra connections. One person

may have a whale for a heart animal and the other may have a whale as an emotional animal. Or one may have a throat animal that is a cat and the other a power animal that is a mouse. So one can spot not only direct relationships but cross-chakra relationships.

Two things emerge from this. The couple is able to focus with greater precision on areas of conflict rather than identifying their relationship in general as being in conflict; they can acknowledge the healthy aspects of the relationship without allowing them to get swallowed up in concern about the conflict. Secondly, it allows them ways of articulating and communicating about their own relative growth, so that they have a more intimate understanding of the changes that occur as their relationship evolves and they each grow.

In use with families this process portrays the true complexity of the family and could perhaps open up some new ways of viewing family dynamics.

Over a year ago Stuart Alpert and Naomi Bressette introduced the Personal Totem Pole work into their curriculum for therapist training at Hartford Family Institute in Connecticut. They have also carried the work to Kansas City and to Germany where Naomi has used the animals successfully in working with issues and dynamics of small groups.

The Personal Totem Pole process is also highly valuable for teenagers as they go through those years of tremendous growth, at which times they may desperately need sources of inner support.

Interest is also high in exploring this work with patients who suffer from particular illnesses, like cancer or aids. Are there any common animal or relationship elements? Can they be effective in healing at the physical level? And is it possible that this process could also help others where the compensation of one function by another is essential, e.g., people with multiple sclerosis or other illnesses.

The journeys and transformations that occur in the inner work are actually contemporary sources of myth and literature, and serve to put us back in touch with a mythology that is vitally alive and personal rather than remote and ancient. It is also a healing mythology. It enables us to recognize that classical and ancient mythology also originated from this lively, personal realm.

We are each a source of literature, it is a living fountain in each of us and not the property of writers. I always encourage my clients to write their imagery stories, either for themselves, or to give to their children, or to present to the larger public in books and articles.

There is also some early work that we would like to resume, work that was underway when I first met the chakra animals. This is work with imagery guides that could help explore particular dimensions.

We had done some initial work getting in touch with Dream Guides. A Dream Guide is an image who can take a person on a journey back through a dream and help them learn and understand the nature of the dream, it's reason for coming, how it was meant to help them learn or grow, and how they should appropriately relate to it. Our initial explorations were fascinating and full of promise.

Teresa and I also did some initial explorations in getting in touch with an imagery guide who could then take one back through a piece of art work that had been spontaneously created as art therapy. This work also is full of potential.

We also wished to explore similar work with guides who could take one through the classical myths and fairy tales, elucidating and expounding on them. Sometimes this has happened spontaneously in the animal work. For example, my sister, Rosalie Douglas, was told by one of her animals that the story of Jack and the Beanstalk was about man's relationship to God, trying to steal the golden eggs rather than learning to live in harmony with Him.

In our culture imagery itself has never been used *systematically* as a tool to help us gain an understanding of our world, yet it could be a method with a value equal to that of the scientific method. It is also evident that we have barely scratched the surface of the potential of imagery for bringing our lives to that fullness and richness that is our fundamental heritage. We hope our work can be one of the doorways which allows entrance.

The animals have grown me deeply, and those with whom I have shared my work have also helped me grow. Each of the people I mention in this book has helped me grow significantly. Each of the workshops I have presented, and each of the clients I have worked with, have been sources of growing for me.

Of my animals, all but one have gone through highly significant changes. My Grounding animal has gone through many transformations beginning with the original rabbit, even at one time having been a giant sandworm from Dune, but ultimately being transformed into the very Earth itself. My Crown animal has changed only once: from the cylinder of golden sunlight into the open sky.

I am deeply honored to be part of the channel by means of which the Personal Totem Pole process has returned. I am aware of the deep involvement of the Native American culture in providing the original foundation for this and in being part of the path by means of which it came to me. One of the commitments I make is to return the chakra animals to Native Americans. I feel that in this we will have begun to come full circle. Our original lack of understanding Native American culture stemmed from an ignorance of our own Being, and healing ourselves can go hand in hand with the healing of our relationship with our Native American hosts. Hopefully the chakra animals can be a healing link in this direction.

Santa Fe, New Mexico
May 22, 1987

References

Blyth, R. H. Zen in Western LIterature and Oriental Classics. New York: E. P. Dutton, 1960.

Eliade, M. Shamanism: Archaic Techniques of Ecstasy. Princeton: Bollingen, 1964.

Gallegos, E. S. Animal imagery, the chakra system, and psychotherapy. J. Transp. Psych., 1983, 15(2), 125-136.

Gallegos, E. S. and Rennick, T. Inner Journeys: Visualization in Growth and Therapy. Great Britain: Turnstone, 1984.

Hillman, J. Re-Visioning Psychology, New York: Harper & Row, 1975.

Krishnamurti, J. The First and Last Freedom. New York: Harper & Row, 1975.

Miller, S. Dialog with the higher self. Synthesis, 1978, 2, 122-139.

Stewart, H. Looking at Indian Art of the Northwest Coast. Vancouver: Douglas & McIntyre, 1979.

Storm, H. Seven Arrows, New York: Ballentine, 1973.

Tedlock, D. The way of the word of the breath. Alcheringa: Ethnopoetics One. 1975, 2, 4-5.

Watkins, M. Waking Dreams, 3rd edition. Dallas: Spring, 1984.